J.K. LASSER PRO
FEE-ONLY
FINANCIAL PLANNING

The *J.K. Lasser Pro* Series

J.K. Lasser Pro Securing the Later Years: Investment Strategies for Retirement and Estate Planning
    David R. Reiser and Robert L. DiColo with Hugh M. Ryan
J.K. Lasser Pro Fee-Only Financial Planning: How to Make It Work for You
    John E. Sestina
J.K. Lasser Pro Preparing for the Retirement Boom
    Thomas Grady

The *Wiley Financial Advisor* Series

Tax-Deferred Investing: Wealth Building and Wealth Transfer Strategies
    Cory Grant and Andrew Westhem
Getting Clients, Keeping Clients
    Dan Richards
Managing Family Trusts: Taking Control of Inherited Wealth
    Robert A. Rikoon with Larry Waschka
Advising the 60+ Investor: Tax and Financial Planning Strategies
    Darlene Smith, Dale Pulliam, and Holland Tolles
Tax-Smart Investing: Maximizing Your Client's Profits
    Andrew D. Westhem and Stewart J. Weissman

J.K. LASSER PRO
FEE-ONLY
FINANCIAL PLANNING
How to Make It Work for You

John E. Sestina, CFP, ChFC

John Wiley & Sons, Inc.
New York • Chichester • Weinheim • Brisbane • Singapore • Toronto

ISBN: 0-471-38808-4

Printed in the United States of America

10 9 8 7 6 5 4 3 2 1

To Bobbi and Alison
To Fred, Beth, and Charlie

Contents

Appendix F   Client Master

Preface

ee-only financial planning is now the fastest-growing segment in the entire financial services industry.

Fee-Only Financial Planning: How to Make It Work for You is a practical, proven, step-by-step guide to making the transition to this profitable profession. It covers the spectrum from the philosophical advantages of fee-only planning to tips on how to set up and manage your office, recruit clients, set fees, and systematize the planning process. This book will enable you to incorporate the enormous technological and educational changes of the past few years and their impact on the system I started building and refining in 1965.

When I taught the first university-level course in personal financial planning in 1969, few had even heard the term. No one could have predicted that fee-only financial planning would be so popular 30 years later.

The first edition of this book was written in 1991. The profession of financial planning has virtually exploded since then:

- From one national professional association—the National Association of Personal Financial Advisors (NAPFA)—with a mere 60 members 10 years ago, the profession has now grown to seven membership organizations in the United States and extensions in 10 other countries. NAPFA, made up exclusively of fee-only financial planners, now has more than 650 members. The recent merger of the International Association for Financial Planning (IAFP) and the Institute of Certified Financial Planners (ICFP) into the Financial Planning Association (FPA) will close the gap and overlap between the two older organizations' 17,000 and 14,000 members, respectively.

- Twenty-one professional designations can be earned by more than 20 job titles dealing with different aspects of the field. More than 33,100 individuals have earned the Certified Financial Planner (CFP) designation from the College for Financial Planning in Denver, Colorado.

- Now, 93 colleges and universities in 32 states prepare students for the profession.

- The profession has grown to the extent that it warrants government regulation from eight agencies at the federal level and four types of oversight bodies in each state.

- As anyone who has surfed the Internet can tell you, countless Web sites market the services of those in the industry seeking to capitalize on the growing popularity of personal financial planning.

Establishing a brand-new profession has been a long, challenging, and rewarding road.

When I started looking for my first client in 1965, financial compensation was a concern. By the early 1970s, I had run the gamut: I had taken commissions only, charged fees and taken commissions, and charged fees and offset them with commissions. I felt compelled to make a decision. Charging fees combined with the sale of products had too much potential for clouding my recommendations. To offer the optimum in nonbiased advice required that I charge fees only.

About that time, I learned that another planner had become successful by charging fees rather than selling products. I met with him and soon discovered a few others who had the same philosophical concerns I did. Out of that core group grew the fee-only financial planning movement and the first national fee-only organization, the National Association of Personal Financial Advisors (NAPFA), founded by Bob Underwood, Jim Schwartz, and me.

One of the objectives of this book is to underscore the many possibilities open to you on entering this profession.

Fee-only financial planning is a client-centered and profitable profession.

When I started out, the conventional wisdom maintained that client-centered and profit-centered were mutually exclusive. In fact, I was told countless times that you simply could not earn a living through fees for service; you had to sell commission products.

My experience has proved that an educated and motivated entrepreneur can become wealthy in his or her own right. The system is simple: Give your clients the objectivity, comprehensiveness, and peace of mind they want. The book has been deliberately structured to demonstrate that the two approaches are actually interdependent: financial planning *must* be client-centered in order to be profitable.

Fee-only financial planning can be accessible to everyone.

In the early years, a common misconception held that only the very wealthy could afford the best in objective and comprehensive advice.

The fact is there is an enormous and largely still-untapped market for fee-only financial planners to serve. Today's consumers are both more affluent and more educated. Thanks also to the technology revolution, they can become much more personally engaged in the planning process. From the exponential growth of day trading to using Quicken on their computers to track the results you produce for them, working with educated and involved clients is always more productive and profitable for both parties.

Making fee-only financial planning accessible on a systematic basis to every American was the foundation for creating the Sestina Network of Fee-Only Financial Planners in 1994. Others have also seen the potential of networking and are following suit.

This book systematizes a wealth of resources to support your successful transition to fee-only financial planning.

Do you need special qualifications to become a good fee-only financial planner? The answer is a resounding "Yes!" In 35 years in the business, I have found three qualities to be absolutely essential: a genuine desire to help people, the ability to listen, and a commitment to lifelong learning.

This book systematically develops the knowledge base that will support building a successful practice on those qualities.

■ Chapter 11, on fees, will give you guidelines on tackling this potentially awkward subject. I'll show you why it's better to bill once a year.

■ Up-to-date information in Chapter 9 on structuring your office covers how to set up and manage your office using the latest in computer and other communications technology. You will know how to minimize cost and maximize results to compete effectively with anyone in the marketplace.

■ This book will serve you and your practice well into the fast-changing future. Important updates will be available on our Web site, www.sestina.com.

■ Results-based marketing is key to your success these days, so an entire chapter is devoted to what works and what doesn't. You will find the spectrum from thought-provoking strategic considerations to brochure copy that has worked to address the concerns from your client's bottom-line perspective, as well as tips on using a low-cost Web site effectively.

Now you are familiar with some of the extraordinary opportunities in fee-only financial planning. Applying the knowledge you acquire from this book will be some of the most rewarding work you ever do.

Acknowledgments

Thanks to the many clients I have had through the years who have provided an opportunity for me to see every combination of financial circumstances and to improve their financial bottom lines and their lifestyles.

I am also deeply appreciative of the sharing among fellow financial planners, particularly the other NAPFA members. We have educated each other as this profession has grown. Special thanks to Margery Wasserman, executive director, NAPFA, as well as Bob Underwood and Jim Schwartz.

A special thanks to Debra Englander, my editor at John Wiley & Sons, as well as the other professionals there: Michael Detweiler, Robin Factor, Greg Friedman, Ann McCarthy, Alexia Meyers, and Mary Todd. It has been a pleasure to work with the staff at Cape Cod Compositors. My thanks also to marketing consultant Sandra S. Nichols, who has worked with me since 1978 to find creative ways to educate consumers that they do indeed have choices in financial planning.

JOHN E. SESTINA
Dublin, Ohio

J.K. LASSER PRO

FEE-ONLY
FINANCIAL PLANNING

Overview of Financial Planning

Before we can cogently discuss fee-only planning as a profession, we need to define the term *financial planning*. In general, financial planning is the *scheduled allocation of a client's resources using the appropriate tools and investment vehicles to best achieve that particular client's fiscal goals and objectives.*

Since each client's goals and objectives will be different, so will each client's ultimate financial plan. Planning is an action-oriented process that requires total input on the part of the client and total dedication on the part of the planner to the client in ascertaining those goals and objectives.

Notice that the definition says the *client's* fiscal goals and objectives, not the financial planner's. The best financial plan for any one client is the one the client wants. You can ascertain a client's true wishes only by listening to what he or she really desires. As a financial planner, you must hone your "people skills" to achieve close communication with your clients.

Let's focus on two more words in the definition: *client's resources*. You will discover early on that your clients' resources are generally quite limited. Unless they are born to great wealth, their major resource is income. They have little or no savings. Their income never seems to be sufficient to meet current needs, let alone create a surplus they can invest for the future. As financial planners, we must continually ask ourselves if our clients' goals are practical and achievable based on those limited resources. In other words, can a client get there from here?

The upshot of all this is that, in many cases, there are just not enough resources left at the end of the allocation period to provide everything our clients want. They may be underutilizing or neglecting the tools already at their disposal. It is your job as a financial planner to decide how these tools should be used. In addition, your clients may be underinsured or overmortgaged, or they may be investing in vehicles inconsistent with their objectives. Furthermore, they may be too liquid (readily convertible to cash), or have a poor ratio of equity to debt, or have gaps that need to be bridged.

The planner's first job in taking on a new client is to secure a comprehensive appraisal of the client's total financial situation. The process of gathering the data in conjunction with your clients helps them realize their true bottom line and view your suggestions in a more objective light when it comes time for implementation. The information you gather at this point must be thorough and accurate. The confidential questionnaire in Appendix A can serve as a guide in this process. Also see Chapter 6, "Establishing a System."

Another part of the definition of financial planning uses the words *scheduled allocation*. These words imply planned specifics, action versus reaction, positive as opposed to negative. Scheduled allocation also means that the plan is implemented as it is supposed to be and within the agreed-upon time frame.

This act of implementation gives you the greatest worth to your clients. It's what makes you different from their other advisors and is what you as a financial planner should do best. Proper implementation means that you and your clients have communicated successfully and that you have added value to their lives.

Here is where the phrase *appropriate tools and investment vehicles* comes into play, and where your expertise as a planner shows up. As you know, there are literally thousands of choices that can be made. It is in the proper manipulation of these choices that planners ply their trade.

Skills of the Successful Financial Planner

All successful financial planners must perfect three types of skills: people (or communications), organizational, and technical skills.

Communications Skills

You can get by if you are a technical dynamo, but you are unlikely to prosper without the requisite people skills. You must achieve as close to total communication with your clients as possible. This is best achieved by listening and qualifying. The more you can develop your people skills, the less likely you are to present a wrong or badly flawed plan.

Remember, it is your job to coordinate and implement all fiscal activity for your clients. If you don't listen properly and don't communicate with them, they can turn to stockbrokers, bankers, or insurance agents for advice. Why do they need you? You are an expensive, added layer they can easily drop if you fail to communicate and find out exactly what they need.

Each client must see that you are adding worth to his or her financial affairs before you can say that you have that person as a client. Other professionals are out there fighting to be your client's most trusted advisor. The only way you can claim that title for yourself is by interacting and communicating with a client regularly.

The planner cannot afford to neglect the development of any lines of communication with the client and his or her spouse. Effective communication must be informative, interpretative, and conclusive. It should ultimately result in action based on those conclusions.

You must first listen to and qualify a client to determine what results he or she wants you to achieve. If you feel the goals stated are impractical or unachievable, you must use your best communications skills to alter the client's perceptions. He or she might feel differently when presented with workable alternatives.

Organizational Skills

You have to be extraordinarily well organized to build any kind of reputation as a fee-only planner. These organizational skills must show up everywhere: in your coordination efforts with other advisors, in your endeavors to run a successful business, in your role as a boss, and in your own personal life. Time is your most precious ally. You must be able to delegate, so you need proficient support personnel. More follows on this subject in Chapter 9.

Technical Skills

Technical skills are clearly necessary if you expect to provide quality service to your clients. You must know how to analyze the data you have gathered, discover deficiencies, and make recommendations to improve a client's financial condition.

Depending on your background, you will lack knowledge in some relevant area of financial planning. If you are deficient in one area (such as tax planning or insurance, for example), there is no reason for concern. Through various courses and seminars geared specifically to the financial planner, you can now learn the technical skills necessary. In the event you have a lingering weakness, you can always hire that expertise. More information on degrees and associations to help you gain this expertise will be discussed in Chapter 4.

The Planner as the Team Coordinator

Financial planners don't work in vacuums. They rely on their clients' other advisors, who were probably providing advice long before the client came to a planner. The financial planner is often compared to the quarterback on a football team, calling and directing the plays. I prefer the coach analogy. Like the coach, the planner sets the game plan, directs each of the players, and is the only one who can credibly coordinate the team of advisors because he or she is not selling anything except planning expertise and an ability to coordinate. Such a planner has no one's interests at heart but the client's.

Regardless of how extensive his or her technical skills may be, the fee-only planner invariably shares responsibility for the development of the plan in one of two ways or a combination of both. He or she either utilizes the specialists a client already has—bankers, attorneys, brokers, insurance agents, or realtors—to fine-tune the plan, or puts them in place himself or herself. The successful fee-only planner will have no shortage of professionals willing to help in developing and implementing the plan, but at the outset it will take all of the planner's people skills to communicate the value of this combined venture to the participants.

The fee-only planner must convince specialists, such as insurance agents, that their time is better spent doing what they do best, namely, designing insurance programs for clients, rather than counseling clients on other financial matters they may not know as much about. It's a matter of specialists using their time efficiently. As the financial planning profession clarifies the roles of general practitioner and specialist, there will be several benefits to both clients and planners.

- First, clients will be less confused as to who does what and what financial planning is, and more people will realize that they can benefit from financial planning. We are in the business of creating lifestyles for our clients, yet only a minuscule percentage of the people who can profit from our services use them.

- Second, the specialists can concentrate their efforts on their areas of expertise instead of trying to master all fields of potential investment.

- Third, fee-based and commission-only planners would do well enough financially working in concert with fee-only planners so that fewer of the non-fee-only planners would be inclined to compete against them. Remember that a fee-based planner charges the client a base fee and then also receives commissions as financial products are sold to the client.

■ Finally, bad planners would be pushed to the side.

Public Perceptions of Financial Planners

As of July 2000, the National Association of Personal Financial Advisors had 690 members (www.napfa.org) and the College of Financial Planning had certified almost 36,000 financial planners (www.cfp-board.org). There are probably thousands more in the United States today who call themselves financial planners, but no one can tell how many of them would meet the required qualifications, if there were any. The situation is improving through the efforts of various industry trade associations to catalog and qualify participants. Unfortunately, that effort is not keeping pace with the growth of the industry.

The public is not sure exactly who is a financial planner and who isn't. Are bankers financial planners? How about insurance agents, securities brokers, or lawyers?

The best thing that can happen to the industry is licensing. The credibility gap will begin to close when universities offer degrees in financial planning and professional associations offer designated credentials based on a certain level of financial planning expertise.

The emergence of the fee-only planner will also help solve the reputability problem. Because the fee-only planner gets paid only for developing and implementing a client's plan, there is little or no chance for a conflict of interest, which is among the most damaging public perceptions facing the industry today.

When people think of financial planning, assuming they understand what it is, they usually think first of commission- or fee-based planners who earn their livelihoods by selling products. Because fee-only planners do not get commissions for implementing plans, they are not obligated to recommend certain products or investment vehicles and therefore should not have conflicts with their clients' other advisors. We fee-only planners must get this perception across not only to the public, but also to those planners contemplating a move into fee-only planning.

The news media have the power to make or break us as a viable profession. When a financial planner does something worth crowing about, the code of confidentiality prohibits him or her from calling a press conference to tell people about it. However, should that same planner do something improper, no such code constrains the client from calling a press conference. Bad news is always bigger than good news. It sells papers and attracts viewers, and that means more money in advertising revenues. Fee-only planners can counteract this tendency to sensationalize our news by communicating with the media. We are the experts in financial planning that reporters look for, and if we make ourselves accessible to them on a regular basis, many of those negative stories may not get written or reported.

The public is confused about who financial planners are because various types of planners portray themselves in contradictory ways. Large banks posture themselves as capable of providing complete financial profiles for their depositors; insurance companies offer full-service investment counseling for their policyholders; and certified public accountants (CPAs), attorneys, and brokers have various attractively packaged programs of comparable content for their clients.

With the evolving complexity of the financial services marketplace in recent years has come a redefinition of the roles of the competitors in it. No longer is it bank versus bank or broker versus broker. Now it's bank versus broker, insurance agent versus accountant, and so forth, for the next investment dollar. It is not fair to say that bankers, brokers, accountants, lawyers, and insurance agents have embraced financial planning solely as a tool to increase the marketability of their principal products or services, but it is certain they would not have embraced it if it did not. These types of planners are product-driven; the fee-only planner is process-driven.

Even large brokerage firms realize the value of fee-only financial planning as they are advertising such services.

Origins of the Fee-Only Planner

The Investment Advisors Act of 1940 provided the regulatory framework for selling financial planning services on a fee basis. However, it took 20 years for that law to be exploited. Some financial planning services were offered in the early 1960s but strictly on a commission basis. It wasn't until around 1970 that the first fee-only planners appeared.

It's interesting to note that the first fee-only planners did not come from the ranks of those who charge a fee for professional services, such as accountants and lawyers, but from individuals with commission backgrounds, primarily insurance agents. Only when the financial planning industry began to take on definition did it begin to evolve into its purest form and appeal to other fee-charging professionals.

Because of the burgeoning financial services industry, commission-oriented planners began to see the need to expand their areas of expertise if they wanted to retain the clientele. Once they achieved the level of competence required for full-service planning, they were faced with deciding whether to make the break from the commission products that had provided their livelihood for so many years.

The most confident of those commission planners made the break and were the first of the fee-only planners. Because they were no longer product-oriented, the rest of the investment community ceased to view them as competitors. Some dismissed them as serious players because they could no longer implement, that is, they had no products to sell. Astoundingly, in some quarters these misconceptions still prevail.

The commission-based planners who went to the edge but declined to make the break have at least learned the value of full-service planning. They always implement in conjunction with their fee-only counterparts.

CHAPTER 2

Advantages of Fee-Only Planning

Before making the move to fee-only planning, weigh the pros and cons of the profession. This chapter lays out the many advantages this branch of planning offers you, your clients, and even the other professionals with whom you come in contact. See Chapter 3 for the other side of the coin.

Advantages to the Client

No Conflicts of Interest

Commission or fee-based planners sell products for which they are compensated. It is impossible for them to do what is best for their clients if they have to squeeze a client's plan into one of the products they sell.

It is much easier to establish the required client-planner trust as a fee-only planner. With no conflicts of interest, you can make it clear to clients that their financial well-being is your paramount concern because it also affects your professional well-being. When clients recognize that they are your sole source of revenue, they understand that you best serve yourself by serving them. They are therefore more likely to trust you and stay with you over the long term.

Having no conflicts of interest is the fee-only planner's greatest marketing tool, and it should be reiterated to clients, prospects, and professional colleagues.

More Opportunities

Your status as a product-free coordinator requires that you be competent to evaluate various investment alternatives. You can gain access to the latest and highest-quality alternatives in three ways: (1) you should have knowledge of them yourself; (2) you can ask the client's specialists to make suggestions; and (3) you can use your own specialists.

Because you as a fee-only planner are not in competition with salespeople, they are more likely to bring their products or investment vehicles to you. If they can convince you of the merit of their products and you recommend those products to clients, the salespeople have saved time and have still earned a commission. The fee-only planner's objectivity becomes an advantage not only to the client, but to the salespeople as well.

As with product diversity, supplier or broker diversity is an important part of the service you supply to clients. Fee-only planners are not registered with brokers or distributors of products, so they can shop around for the best products or services for their clients without being tied to one or two sources that might not have everything they need. Brokers and suppliers who want your business will try to outperform their competition to give you the best service possible. That's good news for you and your clients.

Investment Management

Bad choices do get made, and they affect both client and planner, but as a fee-only planner you have one loyalty: your client. You can follow up to secure the best for your client without jeopardizing your status with any product provider. Because you have no allegiance that could cause you to act defensively, you can seek to right the wrong.

Along the same lines, the fee-only planner is in a better position to monitor an investment on an ongoing basis. Monitoring can mean reviewing the financial information provided by the wholesaler or actually visiting a piece of real estate to check on things. The fee-only planner can do this not only before the client invests, but also, more importantly, after the client has invested. This contrasts sharply with the commission-oriented planner, who needs this time to develop new sales opportunities.

Reduced Costs

Another advantage to the client, and hence to the planner who can point it out to the reluctant prospect, is that the client gets more for less. Not only does he or she receive full service and responsible ongoing maintenance and review, but also the fee-only planner can save commissions for the client.

When negotiating for a product on behalf of a client, a fee-only planner can reduce the total cost of the product by eliminating part of the provider's sales costs. The result is that in most cases, more of the client's money is working in the product. For example, a planner who is buying real estate for a number of clients might be able to negotiate better terms up front because of the absence of a sales commission.

Total Implementation

As noted in Chapter 1, implementation is the scheduled spending and management of a client's resources to make the acquisitions required to put the client's plan into effect. The keys are spending wisely and watching the acquisitions closely. The fee-only planner has more choices available on how to spend than anyone else. Remember, just because we cannot sell does not mean we cannot buy.

Unfortunately, many plans are only partially completed because planners must also be prudent businesspeople. That means spending their time being financially productive. Because commission-oriented planners are also prudent businesspeople, they direct their attention to areas that provide the greatest income for themselves. They might handle products that conflict with their planning duties and overlook other potentially profitable alternatives, much to the detriment of the client.

Deductible Fees

In the great majority of cases, the fees you charge will be tax-deductible for your clients. Ruling 73-13 of the Internal Revenue Service, which refers to Section 212 of the code, states that fees for investment advice are deductible. Since investment advice is often an integral part of our service, the annual fee we charge may be deductible. However, a fee charged for advice on a specific investment, such as the recommendation of a stockbroker or commission-only planner, might not be deductible.

Thus, if the fee charged by a fee-only planner and the commission charged by a planner who is not fee-only are equal, the client is better off going with the fee-only planner because the fee may be partially or entirely deductible and the commission is not deductible under any circumstances. Of course, in order to use this deduction, the fee plus other miscellaneous deductions must exceed 2% of the client's adjusted gross income.

Deductibility is also valuable if financial planning is offered as a fringe benefit or "perk" and is paid for by a client's corporation. The client would then pay taxes, if any, only on the benefit.

Advantages to the Planner

Client Loyalty

The name of the game for the fee-only planner is to keep clients from one year to the next. Because people are loyal to those they trust, if you have earned your clients' trust, they probably will stick with you as long as you do a professional job. They will also tell friends, neighbors, and advisors about your services. That word of mouth will generate more clients.

While it is good for commission and fee-based planners to develop long-term relationships, these relationships are critical to the long-term profitability of fee-only planners. Fee-only planners do not have the residual or renewal income from their first year of work. They can create renewal income only by renewing relationships with the same clients.

Commission and fee-based planners want to have long-term relationships as well, but they don't have as much time to devote to them as fee-only planners do. Product-oriented planners get the bulk of their income from selling products, so they usually decide that it is more profitable to seek a new client to whom they can sell their products than to waste time with a reluctant older client. The fee-only planner has no such luxury.

Ironically, these commission-oriented planners will ultimately have to charge fees, and provide additional services to justify them, if they want to continue working with the same clients. Consequently, they often find themselves evolving into fee-for-services planners, despite the fact that they sold only commission products at the outset.

Less Marketing Required

Once you establish yourself as a fee-only planner, you don't have to do as much marketing as your commission-based colleagues. You will establish long-term relationships rather than a series of one-night stands with your clients. As your practice matures, you may even find you don't have to do any marketing whatsoever. You will only have to replace those clients who die, leave, or are terminated. The time that would have been devoted to marketing can be put to better use increasing your knowledge or your level of service to your existing clients.

Limited Competition

As American consumers learn more about fee-only financial planners, they will want to use their services. There are, fortunately, only a limited number of fee-only planners in comparison to commission or fee-based planners. This means more than enough clients to go around for fee-only planners.

Professional Status

Consumers are used to paying a fee for services rendered. Because fee-only planners charge a fee for services, as do doctors, attorneys, and accountants, they appear more professional than other planners. And, whether it is valid or not, many consumers view people who represent one company or one product as less professional than those who don't.

Other professionals will also look at you as a colleague and not as just another salesperson. That professional image will make it easier for you and the other professionals to work together, and you may even get referrals from them.

CHAPTER

3

Disadvantages of Fee-Only Planning

ee-only planning is not for everyone. If you cannot budget your time and set priorities, forget about becoming a fee-only financial planner. You also need to become knowledgeable in every facet of financial planning and find time to earn a fee practicing what you have learned. Some fee-only planners feel that all other types of financial planners are either dishonest or stupid. This holier-than-thou attitude can be a big disadvantage. There are many capable planners who put together high-quality investment opportunities and offer the best service to their clients. They just have no desire to offer their services for a fee.

No Guarantee for the Client

Clients must be told right from the start that there are no guarantees. Just because you charge a fee doesn't mean that your plan or investment strategies will be infallible. Physicians can't guarantee to cure their patients, and neither can you guarantee that everything you do will be error-free.

There is also no guarantee that the planner will recommend only no-load investments and products. Many times it is appropriate for a fee-only planner to recommend a commission vehicle such as life insurance. This may sound like an uncomfortable compromise to the purist, but it must be put into perspective. If, for example, you recommend that a client have a will drawn up, the attorney who does the job must be paid, as should the insurance agent who provides a top-notch insurance package. Should you deny your client the best coverage just because the agent gets a commission?

Finally, there is no guarantee that you will be successful as a fee-only planner. Because of the increasingly high demand for fee-only planners, you might get off to a great start, but, as with any new business venture, you could ultimately fail.

You Must Service What You Sell

As a fee-only planner, you have one great disadvantage over commission-based professionals: You are totally responsible for the whole package you design.

Just about everyone knows an insurance salesperson who is super at selling policies but, once the policy is sold, provides less than vigorous service to the policyholder. The policyholder is serviced through other divisions within the company such as the claims or renewal department. The insurance company attends to the needs of the policyholder, and the salesperson is back on the street selling more policies. The agents are expected to provide service only to the extent that they can sell additional coverage to clients. The company wants them selling policies because it's only through sales that the agents and the company make their money.

Fee-only planners are at the disadvantage of having to provide total service and sales. Their incentive to do so must be that only then can they provide clients with maximum service. Fee-only planners must not only sell their services, they must also accept responsibility for assuring the services of all plan participants in a timely fashion. This is the essence of implementation—of putting the plan into action. The planner monitors the progress of the plan and provides maintenance through the specialists at the proper times.

You Are Selling an Intangible

Another disadvantage is that you are selling a service that is difficult to describe to potential clients. Most other professionals they deal with represent a tangible product or service.

Earlier I used the analogy of the team coach to describe the planner's role. The coach leads the team and calls the plays and is ultimately responsible to the owner. That's the concept you have to sell to potential clients. You are the only member of the financial team who can be the coach with nothing but the "team owner's" (the client's) best interests at heart.

You Fail to Develop Sales Skills

If you can't market, you will be out of business. Part of marketing is selling. Some fee-only planners believe clients will run to their doors just because they are fee-only. The better mousetrap theory is misleading. Many good ideas have gone by the wayside because no one could sell them.

Fee-only planners are concerned about looking like commission planners. Therefore, they do not develop sales skills. This mistake is due to a misunderstanding of quality selling. Remember, all professionals—doctors, accountants, and others—sell.

In fee-only planning, you must know how to sell the benefits of fee-only financial planning. You must learn how to quote your fees, handle client objections, and close the sale.

The National Association of Personal Financial Advisors (NAPFA) has a manual developed to assist you with this aspect of needed technical skills. Read books that teach selling skills. You will also learn a great many people skills from these books.

You Receive No Subsidy

Unlike their commission counterparts, fee-only planners have no subsidy. As in any business, adequate capitalization is a requirement for long-term success. Unfortunately, many people are coming to the fee-only planning business unprepared to face reality. Like the shoemaker whose children go barefoot, they are too busy taking care of clients' needs to attend to their own.

If you haven't provided yourself with enough funds to start and keep your practice going for a few years, you may not make it.

When you make the break from commission to fee-only status, you forfeit the safety of working for or with someone else. The fee-only purist, generally entrepreneurial by nature, is not always geared to be the detail person he or she will need to be when on his or her own. Yet, if you want to succeed in this business, you will have to realize that no one will attend to your needs now but you. You must prepare yourself to take advantage of all opportunities. If you are a true entrepreneur, you will be able to spot them. The challenge will be in using them. This will involve things you might not be used to doing.

For starters, as a newly minted fee-only planner you must find a new office, locate a capable support staff, procure the needed equipment such as computers, and acquire important information sources such as magazines, newsletters, and other industry publications you need in order to do a good job for clients. All of this, especially the hiring of a support staff, is very expensive.

There are no hard-and-fast rules on how all this can be done. The fee-only planner must do it by the seat of his or her pants while at the same time trying to drum up business to pay for it all. This is not meant to scare away potential fee-only planners but rather to give them a realistic view of what's in store.

You Must Attract New Clients

As a novice fee-only planner, you probably will not have a built-in client base. You might have one or two clients from previous commission days who have followed, but they will not be enough to keep you going for any length of time. Remember it takes time to build a successful practice by attracting new clients. It will take time for you to build your credibility and credentials.

In the beginning you will spend much of your time learning. You will have to work out how to fit this time in while you are soliciting new clients. When you are doing comprehensive planning, you will discover gaps in your skills and knowledge. If you can attract a roster of loyal, outstanding clients relatively quickly, you will be the exception and not the rule. Of course, the longer it takes to procure those clients, the more capitalization you will need to tide you over.

Your job of attracting new clients is complicated by the fact that as a fee-only planner you have to tell potential clients right from the start things they don't want to hear. People don't want to be told that they are even more in need of professional assistance than they thought, especially when they find out that they are going to have to become heavily involved in the process. And don't forget that their peers and their coterie of professionals are likely to reinforce that reluctance.

Here are three typical examples of potential clients and the kinds of difficulties you will encounter trying to sell them your services.

1. The client has been doing quite well to this point. He or she has been very lucky on a speculative venture and is resistant to reinvesting profits defensively.

2. This individual is so committed to low-risk ventures that he or she may resist aggressive maneuvers to the point of stagnation to avoid any possible chance of loss.

3. The potential client's finances are in such disrepair that it will take you years to get him or her back on the right track, but the client wants quick results.

You Must Create the Want

All beginning fee-only planners have a difficult time creating the need or want for their services in potential clients. Many people need help but are afraid to seek it for a variety of reasons. Planners are hired to plan positive action for profit, not to react negatively. They must act defensively to safeguard against losses, but they must never be negative.

However, people are both reactionary and negative much of the time. They fear both failure and success, and they are impulsive. How many prospective clients have you lost over the years because, even though every knowledgeable source advised them to take one course of action, they talked to their barbers or golf partners and then reneged?

Sure, you "had them sold," only they didn't buy. Everything "sold" is not always "bought." Those of you with a lot of sales experience know this happens often. For the fee-only planner, it means a well-conceptualized plan gone unimplemented. You analyze why, and then proceed with greater wisdom and resolve.

When you approach prospects to become clients, they will probably want to say no. They will resent the fact that you know more about something than they do, and they will be unhappy that they need your services in the first place. You will have to think about what strategies you can use to create the want in these people.

However, if prospects approach you, then things change. When they have taken the initiative, they feel they are in control and that you need them as clients. It's the difference between creating a want and satisfying a need, between a salesperson and an order taker. Let them think it's their idea, but you must determine how to gain control. Control on your part is a vital element in a successful financial-planning experience.

Still a Young Profession

Financial planning is still in its infancy as a profession, and fee-only planning is even younger. As a result, there is a shortage of information regarding fee-only planning. Only now are some financial publications beginning to realize that we even exist. Until the difference between fee-only and fee-based planners is clarified, consumers will make decisions with inadequate or incorrect information. This confusion could cause consumers to choose fee-based planners because they think those services are less expensive.

Fee-only planning is a new field within a new industry playing for enormous stakes and pretty much unfettered by government regulation. After a generation, it still has not been properly conceptualized to the public it is meant to serve. The competition runs the gamut from cottage to conglomerate, from pretender to planner extraordinaire, and the ball has only begun to roll.

Fee-only planners will emerge as the beacon of this new profession because of their objectivity and individuality. These two values must be communicated to the general public. Our clients are our forum, and our performance as the specialist's specialist will build our reputation from within.

But much more is required. Fee-only planners must command the respect of the varied professionals with whom they compete. They need to convince bankers, brokers, lawyers, insurance agents, and accountants that they can all reap more benefits for themselves and their clients by working together than they can by opposing one another.

Obviously, the best time to do this is when no particular client is involved, but that is both difficult and time-consuming. It's a lot easier to communicate your objectivity when nothing is at stake, but it is also harder to gain access to the required audience. Once you get these people to accept the idea that it will benefit their clients to use your services as a fee-only planner with them involved as specialists, you have turned the corner. Now if you produce, you will not only survive, but you will flourish.

Seek Out a Mentor

You will be well served to find a mentor who can guide you through the rough spots. Find someone who is where you want to be and ask whether he or she will help. Please be aware of more than the external trappings of success. Your mentor should have similar qualities and personality to yours. Read books on mentoring to help you choose.

Making the Transition

Few financial planners start off as fee-only practitioners. They generally come from another line of work that may be related to fee-only planning. Many are currently operating as product or service providers; these are the salespeople, attorneys, insurance agents, bankers, securities brokers, and accountants. Others come from unrelated fields. I am aware of a few who have even become planners because they were frustrated as clients and felt they could do better. However, an ever-increasing number are becoming financial planners directly out of college.

Six Questions for the Would-Be Planner

Depending on the background of the potential fee-only planner, the transition will vary. There are, however, a number of similarities that will apply to all. Every potential fee-only planner must answer the following questions:

1. Should I make the transition?

2. How do I get started?

3. How do I implement?

4. How do I find investments, products, and specialist advisors?

5. What kind of clients do I want to serve?

6. How do I know this business is for me?

Should I Make the Transition?

This is the most fundamental question of all. If you can't answer with a clear "I should," then you shouldn't. Fee-only financial planning is no different from any other profession or business when it comes to the business side of things. The same advice you would give a client about starting a new business applies to you as well. Are there services you want to provide that you cannot in your present job or profession? Do you want to invest more for your clients and do comprehensive planning? What services do you want to offer? Do your clients have unmet needs in parts of their financial lives that you cannot meet right now?

No business is easier to get into than fee-only planning, but none is harder to build. In general, you have to go into this profession with a positive attitude. You must be willing to invest in people, education, and equipment. You must be willing to assume financial risks, especially for the first year or two, while you build a clientele. Initially, you may not be able to afford an impressive office or top-notch support people. But if you stay around for five years or so, you will probably have it made. You will eventually find your niche in the profession.

For some reason, people considering a financial planning career often have higher expectations than they would for any other profession. Many potential fee-only planners assume that they will make a six-figure income in the first year. This is an absurd and dangerous notion. It's absurd because it just won't happen, and it's dangerous because those who don't attain that income will appear as failures to others who hold that standard. Remember it takes time to build any business. Are you willing to make a commitment to stick with this venture until you succeed? Depending on your strengths and weaknesses, this transition could take several years to be profitable. However, even if you suffer a large drop in income the first few years, the long-term benefit is worth it.

How Do I Get Started?

You get started the same way you would if you were starting any other business. You read everything you can get your hands on. There are books, magazines, and newsletters that will help you keep up with what's going on and what you must know.

Talk to successful people in the fee-only business. Ask them what they like and dislike about the business. What big problems did they have when they began? How long did it take them to become successful?

How Do I Implement?

Without question, the most important part of the financial planning process is implementation. Without it, you are of no use to the client. To implement properly, surround yourself with outside experts whom you trust. The development of this team will take time and education, but, properly chosen, the team will educate you and serve your mutual clients. This practical experience will be far more beneficial than hours of textbook study.

Remember, though, you are seeking to become a generalist, not a specialist. At first, you might have to work all day and study all night to learn what you must know. If you are reasonably intelligent, you will grow into the job.

How Do I Find Investments, Products, and Specialist Advisors?

Again, the answer is time. Research who in your locale can be trusted in the various areas your clients might need. Then you can align yourself with outside experts in various disciplines such as:

- Estate planning—an attorney

- Taxation—an attorney or an accountant

- Benefit plans—an actuary or other expert

- Pension plans—an accountant, attorney, or other expert

- Insurance—an agent

- Investments—an investment advisor or securities broker

- Real estate—a real estate broker or an attorney for the purchase or sale

By asking them to review your plan and make recommendations, you will learn from experts the kinds of specific actions to take with a particular client. Their input will help you develop a format for your financial plan. You will have to pay the specialists to review your plans, but you can build these costs into your fees.

What Kind of Clients Do I Want to Serve?

Recognizing that you may have to settle for what you get when you start out, it is still important to target your market. You will be happier working with the kind of people you prefer, and you will probably do a better job for them. Try to determine whether you prefer working with a certain occupational group or with people who have a certain net worth or income level. Do you already have a customer base from which you can draw your early clients? More on targeting clients in Chapter 7.

Once you determine the type of clientele you wish to attract, develop procedures and services that will help you find them. You need a business plan geared to that clientele. The plan should cover several areas.

The financial component of the plan requires more elaboration. In serving clients, we ask them to perform certain financial exercises that they find cumbersome, such as budget or cash flow projections. In analyzing an investment, we ask the promoter or broker to prepare financial projections. In starting our fee-only business, it is equally important for us to spend adequate time preparing financial projections. Many aspiring planners fail to prepare a complete business plan. Without this plan, they are never sure how much money is necessary to succeed. They run their practice on a shoestring and struggle more than they should. Valid, accurate projections can reduce the novice planner's fear of failure. There are now inexpensive computer programs to assist you in the development of your plan.

You will need to express your vision that you see for your company. Make certain you list specific goals, including number of clients and revenue. Examine the market, including trends you feel are important to your new venture. In your plan, always consider the client needs and characteristics as you perceive them. Evaluate the competition in your area. Compare your strengths and weaknesses to theirs. Develop a strategy that is right for your business. In your plan, position yourself successfully against the competition by a realistic analysis. Your plan should include a marketing strategy and send a consistent message to all. You will need to evaluate key personnel, facilities, and so forth as an important part of your plan. Finally, run the numbers.

How much capital do you need to start your practice? There is no rule of thumb. You should prepare a 12-month cash flow projection much like the one included in Appendix C as well as a 5-year cash flow projection to show how your business will grow. Of course, these cash flow projections will include business income and expenses such as:

Facilities

   Rent

   Office space requirements

Marketing

   Business cards

   Yellow Pages

Professional support

   Secretarial

   Financial analyst

Attorney

CPA

Back office support

Equipment and furniture

Computers

Fax

Printer

Furniture

Software

Word processing

Spreadsheet

PowerPoint

Financial planning

Internet

E-mail

Bookkeeping

Personal information manager (Outlook, Day-Timer, etc.)

Analytical

Portfolio management

Maintenance and renewal

Finances

Debt payment

Registration and compliance costs

Memberships

Continuing education

Subscriptions

Insurance

Office

Liability

Life

Disability

Property and casualty

Workers' compensation

Office supplies

Printing

Postage

Travel

However, remember to include your household needs as part of your overall financial evaluation. Lack of money for your family can be the pressure that causes your practice to fail, especially if you have dependents. If you do not have sufficient capital to fund the first few years, you may have to borrow it. You will need a relationship with a banker who appreciates you and your business plan and will lend you the funds. In addition, an experienced banker can be a valuable resource for your company. He or she can identify holes in your plan you may have overlooked. It also would be advisable at this early stage to develop a board of advisors you feel have insight about you, your shortcomings, and experience in financial services.

Assuming you are starting on your own, you will want a simple business structure. A sole proprietorship is probably the simplest and least expensive to operate. However, a corporation or a limited liability company offers some liability protection and tax planning opportunities. You will have additional paperwork and record keeping with these entities. In fact, those requirements may prove helpful in treating your business like a business. An attorney and CPA will prove helpful in making this decision. Again, I would invite them to serve on your advisory board.

How Do I Know This Business Is for Me?

Not everyone is cut out to be a financial planner, let alone a fee-only planner. To assess your potential, answer the following questions. If you are concerned about your ability to evaluate yourself, discuss these questions with your spouse or a trusted advisor.

- Do I see myself as a professional advisor?

- Do I enjoy helping people reach their goals?

- Do I enjoy wrestling with both sides of an issue to find an unbiased answer?

- Do I enjoy research and learning?

- Do I enjoy and am I good at in-depth analysis?

- Am I comfortable being the catalyst?

- Am I willing to put in the time and effort necessary to attract clients?

- Am I able to deal with a considerable amount of paperwork?

- Do I have good contacts with other professionals?

- Am I willing to keep educating myself?

- Why do I want to be a fee-only financial planner?

If you answer these questions truthfully and the answers are satisfactory, you will know for sure whether you want to be a fee-only financial planner.

Where Are You Coming From?

The level at which you enter fee-only planning dictates what you must do to become successful.

From Unrelated Fields

If you are coming from an unrelated field or are just out of school, you will first need to develop your credentials. You might have to go back to college for undergraduate or graduate work in financial planning. More and more schools are offering degrees in financial planning. Some of these include Wright State, Purdue, Brigham Young, Golden Gate, Arizona State, Georgia State, Sarasota, Drake, Cal State at Fresno, San Diego State, and the American College in Bryn Mawr, Pennsylvania, which offers a master's degree in financial services.

You must acquire both the ChFC (Chartered Financial Consultant) and CFP (Certified Financial Planner) designations. That will take a few years. For more information on how to achieve these designations, contact the American College, Student Services Department, 270 Bryn Mawr Avenue, Bryn Mawr, PA 19010, (215) 526-1000; or College for Financial Planning, 9724 East Hamden Avenue, Denver, CO 80231, (303) 755-7101.

To accelerate your professional growth, join the National Association of Personal Financial Advisors (NAPFA), which caters exclusively to fee-only planners. Contact the organization at National Association of Personal Financial Advisors, 1130 Lake Cook Road, Suite 105, Buffalo Grove, IL 60089.

Your next major need is experience working in the field, but this might prove difficult to come by. Since more fee-only firms are small and generally have the principals as consultants, it might be hard to break in. Frankly, it is not necessary to work for a fee-only firm to gain financial planning experience. You can learn the fee-only part by networking with other fee-only planners.

The best solution is to find an internship program with a firm willing to take you on. You won't earn much as an intern, but you will learn a great deal. Unfortunately, internship programs are few and far between. Neither the College for Financial Planning nor the American College sponsors any. My attempt at providing this entry opportunity was to create the Sestina Network of Fee-Only Financial Planners.

If an internship is not available, you can participate in a training program offered by a large securities brokerage firm or insurance company. The major risk here is that you might not be able to switch your thinking to commission-oriented planning, or, worse, you might become indoctrinated with that philosophy.

As the new kid on the block, you will be more dependent than ever on whatever networks or associations you already have. These include local charitable, service, or fraternal organizations as well as professional organizations such as NAPFA.

Should you begin on your own right from the start, don't try to reinvent the wheel. Use existing computer programs and systems until you feel you need to develop your own. Software packages such as Quicken, Money, and products emanating from the Bureau of National Affairs, Inc. (BNA) can be adapted quite easily to your individual requirements. Practice management aids are also available.

From Commission Sales

Many people enter fee-only planning via the commission sales route. They generally have been insurance agents or stock and bond brokers. Presumably, the transition here is easier because of related experience. There are, however, some additional considerations to be aware of that can be either positive or negative in nature.

You already have an existing client base, and this is certainly a big plus in terms of immediate business as well as referrals. You might want to discuss the possible change with your best clients to gain their input. You could be very surprised at how helpful they can be. Then, having dealt with your best clients, visit with the rest of your clients and explain how they will benefit from the transition you are making. Also, explain what your billing procedure will be. You might want to meet with these clients individually, but group meetings take less time and can be just as beneficial.

To demonstrate how your old clients will benefit from your new profession, you can develop a financial plan for them because you are already familiar with their personal financial situations. If you have not been doing a plan for them, a total plan will impress them. If you have been planning for them, your new perspective should win them over.

When coming from a commission background, you need to evaluate the economics of your transition differently than other non-fee-only planners do. In your previous position you may have had some economic support that is probably no longer available. For instance, you will have to consider whether you can afford the loss of the back-office support you once had. Will the loss of the advertising and marketing offered by the main product you sell have a negative impact on you? Will your new enterprise be sufficiently profitable to replace the expenses that were paid for before? It's important to protect yourself from losing any renewal income to which you might be entitled. These renewals can help finance your new venture. You will find that even if you must forsake this stream of income of commissions, trail fees, or insurance renewals, it will not be as painful as you anticipated.

You will need to divest yourself of other entanglements. Perhaps you own a brokerage firm on the side. Maybe you have an entity that serves as a general partner in investments you have brokered or personally structured. These will have to be sold or closed. You need not necessarily cancel your licenses. In some states you will be required to have a license to be a fee-only planner. You may need to retain these licenses to continue to receive renewal income. Are there arrangements you must make with your former broker-dealer? What about trailing commissions? If you have noncompetition agreements, are there any points for negotiation?

Despite the fact that you have credentials in other areas, it will still be necessary to establish credentials in financial planning. This means both a ChFC and a CFP. You will also have to change your mind-set. That means focusing on the needs of the client rather than fitting the client to the product. This could be the hardest part of your transition.

From Other Financial Services Professions

If you have come out of the financial services industry, you probably have an existing client base on which you can build your fee-only practice. Everything we discussed with regard to commission-oriented planners applies to you as well.

You, too, have areas from which you must divest yourself. Unlike the sales-oriented individual, you had another, separate profession. If you don't get rid of the other business, it will always take priority. For example, if you continue practicing as a CPA, tax deadlines will interfere with your new business.

A unique challenge you must deal with is making specific recommendations. Be prepared to accept liability for making specific rather than general recommendations in all areas, including investments.

You will need to make a philosophical change as well. The report is not the primary product, as it was with the tax return or financial statement. Implementation is the most important part of the service. You will need to develop a personal interest in the client rather than in the entity the client owns.

You will have to convince your clients that this move will benefit them for several reasons. You will improve your service to them at a comparable cost to what they currently pay. They will have a wider range of financial products because you are no longer limited to offering only commission-generating products. This flexibility is a tremendous benefit to your clients, a benefit you must be sure they understand. Explain that by being compensated only by fees, you are able to expand your product list to include all investment options, insurance products, bank instruments, and anything else imaginable. Remind the clients how much in fees and commissions your previous relationship generated. Then help the clients understand the obvious charges and fees they will now pay you. Show them how much you expect to charge them over the next 24 months. This will take some class. Even with all this explanation, you should expect to lose many of your existing clients.

Regardless of your prior profession, you are now taking advantage of an exploding one. Fee-only financial planning will be the ultimate method of practicing, and the experiences you bring and your contribution to this emerging profession will undoubtedly prove satisfying.

Succeeding with the Small Client

When you first start out, it is unrealistic to assume that you will work only with top executives and millionaires. You may, with a little luck and a lot of competence, work yourself into that position, but your first clients will probably have an income of $50,000 or less.

For purposes of this discussion, people who make less than $50,000 a year will be considered "small." They probably have only a few thousand dollars of assets, and most of their future earning potential is tied up in the company where they work. They could be newly minted doctors or lawyers or up-and-coming businesspeople who still have a way to go in their careers. On the other hand, they could be people who are nearing retirement and are concerned about their standards of living during those golden years. Small clients might also be young couples who have not yet begun a family but want one.

This is an ideal market for the novice fee-only planner to tap. Why? First, the demand is there. Older, more experienced planners who are interested in high-asset, high-income clients probably already turned them away. Now they become fair game for you.

Second, you can initially perform fewer tasks for them because they lack the resources that full service entails, and you may actually be able to do more for them. These people are just putting their financial plans together, so they need a good deal of guidance. Since there is less for you to do as a planner, you should be able to provide it. If you do, these clients are much more likely to give you referrals than their wealthy counterparts. They are usually enthusiastic about breaking new ground for themselves, and they probably will feel more comfortable dealing with you as a relative newcomer to financial planning than with a more experienced planner.

Third, since you do less work for them, you can charge them a smaller fee than a more experienced planner could. This will give you more time to learn the craft and develop a system. Your main job will be data gathering rather than implementation. You will want to develop a cash flow regimen and a plan that properly utilizes their limited financial resources. These are the tasks that distinguish you from the commission-only or fee-based planner, and they should form the basis of your philosophy as a fee-only planner. As your clients' plans develop, it becomes necessary for you to perform more tasks on their behalf, but by then you'll be ready because you will have grown with them.

Fourth, like it or not, you have a good deal in common with these entry-level clients. You are both just getting into real financial planning—they as clients, you as planner. The more cash flow projections you do, the better you will be able to handle your own.

You may not impress many heavy hitters operating out of a two-room office with one all-purpose assistant, but fledgling clients will relate to you. Therefore, it's more realistic to pursue them. They will be thankful they are not paying for a riverfront suite and an entourage of office aides. Let them be impressed with your service.

Fifth, as you and your firm grow, you have a way to train your new associates. Should you later decide to deal with wealthier clients, you can turn over the new or smaller clients to an associate. This gives him or her some practical experience and allows you to expand your business without losing the people who helped get you there.

How Can I Service the Small Client and Still Be Profitable?

Initially, you have to get your own house in order. Start by doing exactly what you would first do with a client—a cash flow projection. This will help you determine how much your lifestyle will be affected by this move you are making. As discussed earlier, create a 12-month and 5-year cash flow projection for your business. If you are not willing to do that simple thing for yourself, you probably can't help your clients in the long run because you won't be around.

The cash flow projections will show exactly how much income you will need to get by. You will probably then have to cut back on your lifestyle. You are not going to walk into fee-only financial planning and become a millionaire—because most planners, even those working with the high rollers, aren't millionaires. You can make a very nice six-figure income working with smaller clients, but you won't do that, either, until you have been at it for a few years. As a rank beginner, you probably won't make more than $25,000 or $30,000 your first year, but it won't take long to get to that magic six-figure mark if you are competent and give your clients top-notch service.

The next thing you will find out in doing your cash flow projection is your overhead for the practice. For smaller clients you don't need a raft of office computers or expensive prints on the walls. You need a simple "lean and mean" office. Remember, you're not in the business of impressing your clients, but of serving them.

Once you're in business for yourself, you will quickly find out how to save money on things like phone bills and office supplies. You probably will want to invest in a computer, but you can certainly pick one up for $2,000 or maybe less. You can hire an assistant to handle your calls, greet your incoming clients, and do your typing and filing. At this point, only one person is necessary. Many of your professional colleagues can tell you the going rate for a secretary in your locale.

You might also consider setting up your office in your home. Many planners do it, especially beginners. You will be spared the high rents of downtown office buildings, and you can get a tax deduction for a home office. By having your office in your home, you may pull in neighbors as clients who might be intimidated by a downtown location.

How Long Will It Take You to Get Started?

Your cash flow planning should help you decide how long it will take you to get going. Assume that you can get by on $30,000 the first year. If you decide on a fee of $500 for a plan, you need 60 clients to achieve that goal. Sixty clients may sound like a lot, but it really isn't. If you're going after the $50,000-a-year earner, you will have plenty of potential clients to choose from if you market yourself properly. Your cash flow projections might also tell you that your overhead will be $10,000 in your first year. If that's so, then you need 20 more clients. Thus, to succeed the first year (which we all know is the most difficult year for any business) you will need 80 clients.

How Much Time Does a Client Take?

If you have never planned before, this could be your big bugaboo. How much time should I spend with clients so that I get everything I need, and they feel satisfied that I have spent enough time with them?

In my experience, you should spend 25 hours a year on this type of client. That time should break down this way: It will take you two hours to sell him or her on hiring you; four hours on data gathering; two more hours for organizing data; another two hours preparing the appropriate recommendations based on the data; four hours for your presentation to the client of the recommendations and one hour for miscellaneous duties. That totals 15 hours. I have allowed 10 hours of overlap for inexperienced planners. That $500 figure I used for the fee was a working figure. There's nothing to say you can't get $750 or $900 for your plan. The number that is usually used to calculate these fees is 2,000 total hours worked in a year. If you "bill out" 1,500 of those hours on fee work, that will leave you 500 hours to devote to the rest of your clients, your business, and more marketing.

If you spend more than 25 hours per client per year, you are probably spending too much time. You have to analyze where you are going, and that involves taking a look at your system for dealing with these clients.

How Much Should I Invest in the Business?

The next thing you need to examine is how much total investment you are willing to make in the business. You might have to borrow money, but that's true of most entrepreneurs. There's nothing to be frightened of. As you well know, businesses borrow money every day. You also might have to use all of your existing savings. You might have to do as I did and cash in your retirement program from your previous employer. I was a teacher, and when I left the profession, I withdrew all $1,300 I had accumulated to begin my financial planning practice. It was risky, but it worked out all right and I'm glad I did it.

How much you end up investing depends on how well you do. Play it by ear. If you make money in your first few months in the business, you might consider pouring most of it back into your practice to pay for necessities. Of course, if you have borrowed a sufficient amount (again, you have calculated this by using your cash flow projections), you may not have to put anything back.

Developing a System to Save Time

You might well be asking yourself, how can I provide full service to these clients in just 25 hours? You can. It just means using your time efficiently and developing a system that can be applied to all your clients, small or large.

Here are some ideas on developing an efficient system for the smaller client:

■ Because smaller clients have fewer resources to allocate, there is less reason to meet face-to-face with them or their advisors. Try to conduct most of your business over the telephone. If a client has some major life changes that require a good deal of your time, you can charge for that on an hourly basis. You can make your small clients responsible for implementation. You don't have to meet with their advisors, but you can direct implementation over the phone.

■ You can spend less time developing the plan presentation because small clients have less data to gather and organize. An information form mailed to the client prior to your initial meeting should contain most of the information you'll need to do a good job.

■ Once set up, the plan for a small client will require less maintenance than one for a larger client. Since you won't be constantly recommending changes and updates to the client's investments, you need not contact him or her so often.

■ Another time-saver involves data gathering. Consider doing it with the client. While entering the data on your computer, you can get the answers to questions as you go along. Clients will prefer this face-to-face contact. They will feel like they are getting more value when they are sitting with the key person, and that person is taking the time to enter the data and start planning their cases while they are there.

■ If you have an investment philosophy, write it down and have it ready to send out to prospective clients along with your information questionnaire. You can instruct the client to read the information before he or she comes to see you for the first time. That way you won't need a long discussion about your investment philosophy during the first meeting.

   That investment philosophy piece can also screen out potential clients who might be incompatible with your way of doing things. If a potential client is a risk taker and you are of a more conservative turn of mind, it's better to find out before the client wastes time coming to see you.

■ You can have a single annual presentation as opposed to two or three, which are normally required with high-income clients.

■ You can also save time by doing very little writing. If a client wants to know about annuities, the insurance companies have better brochures on the subject than you can supply. Brokerage firms have similar information booklets on securities, and there are some excellent books available on personal finance that you can recommend. Writing takes time, and it's expensive, particularly if you use a computer. Any writing you do should be of a standardized nature.

■ One piece of writing you must do is a letter detailing exactly what went on at your last meeting with the client. By doing so, you can avoid arguments or a confrontation at your next meeting about what was decided. You can buy a small pocket dictating machine and dictate the letter while the client is still there at the end of the session. That way, the client can clear up any misapprehensions on the spot. Today, you may choose to type your memo in front of the client and share it with him or her by means of another computer monitor. Then you can print it out at the conclusion of your meeting and give it to the client.

■ Mutual funds are usually suitable for the smaller as well as the larger client. The funds are simply purchased. If you routinely recommend certain no-load funds, order a big pile of their prospectuses, and when it comes time to implement, you'll have one ready to go. You may not qualify for the services of a Charles Schwab or Waterhouse, though, due to the minimum size of investments they may require.

See Chapter 6 for more information on establishing a system.

Attitude Adjustments

Just as the biggest challenge facing a small client is changing one's attitude on making a start toward financial independence, it is also wise to review your own preparedness to deal with such clients. Although you use the same system for all your clients, they do not adhere to the same schedule in getting processed. Nor are they all responsive to the same motivational chord. There are general parameters to observe, but no one factor will more greatly influence their attitude than your attitude. You must examine your own motives for devoting a portion of your practice to these clients and come to terms with the results. Failure to do so will adversely affect your relationships with these individuals. You need to have your own plan in place before you set out to prepare plans for others.

You can't attract what isn't there, so begin your analysis by determining what types of clients may be available to you. You will find that the only clients available everywhere are the small clients. The sooner you accept them for what they may mean to you, the sooner the value of your services will become apparent to them—and to others.

Utilize all the people skills you have accumulated over the years to make all your clients feel they are special to you, that you are concerned about them simply because they are your clients, the backbone of your profession. If they are to respect your judgment, you need to show them that you respect their situations and are accepting responsibilities along with them.

If you are a beginner, you can't afford to pass up the opportunity to teach and learn from entry-level clients. You won't become successful overnight, but you will become more successful every night, and that, after all, is the name of the game.

Establishing a System

If you have ever observed CPAs at work, you know that they all follow a standard practice or process each time they do an audit or tax return. As a fee-only planner, do the same thing—develop a system. The routine must become second nature if you want to give your clients the full service for which they are paying.

Your system is a way of organizing how you do your work, how you pursue the process. Although organization is the most vital element of a system, the system itself is much more than organization. It has to work for everyone involved in the planning process—the client, the spouse, the advisors, you, your staff, your specialists, the entire network. It must be structurally rigid (yet internally flexible), simple, and set up to facilitate refinement. Once it is in place, do not deviate from your system. The sooner you devise an effective and efficient system, the sooner you establish yourself as a fee-only planner.

My system has evolved to the point where, in retrospect, I can say about 25% of it grew from my technical skills, 25% from organizational skills, 25% from people skills, and 25% from teaching skills. It has worked for me for more than 30 years. Some of my techniques don't work for some of my peers, but if they are successful, their techniques accomplish the same things, and so will yours. My system has been effective enough to allow a firm to prosper even after I have left the firm. Some of the largest firms using the system continue to prosper with it.

Every plan must follow the same procedure to afford you control, allow you to be thorough, and help you to be organized. These are the three basic elements of a system. After you complete the transition to fee-only status, don't do any more plans than you can accommodate within your system, and add more clients as you improve the system.

I started out as small as the smallest, grew to be the largest, and am now in a position that allows me to be among the most selective, and I have used the same system throughout. It is rigid and requires strict adherence to specifics, and it is also flexible and accounts for economic volatility and human nature. Furthermore, it is simple. Everything needed is used; nonessentials are discarded. My system has undergone so many refinements over the years that it's sometimes tough to recognize, but it still accomplishes the same three things. When we begin a plan, I'm in charge. All the information is collected, verified, and laid out in good order.

How a System Helps You

A good ongoing system will save you time, will help you do your job more efficiently, and will impress your client. If the system functions well, it should give the appearance of a well-oiled machine. You are, in the client's eyes, well organized, and that enhances your credibility. It also reassures the client that you know what you are doing. Even if you have been at financial planning only a short time, a well-developed system will make you look like you've been at it for a long while.

More than anything else, a system forces a strict process of organization on you. If you can organize your workload, you will use your time to its maximum efficiency. And if you maximize your efficiency, you will be more profitable because you are devoting fewer hours to making the same amount of money. Those hours you save can be used for other profit-making endeavors such as finding new clients.

A system can help you retain clients for the long term because once they are organized using your system, and once they understand it, they will be reluctant to move on to someone else who might do things differently.

How a System Helps Your Clients

Once your clients start using your system, they will benefit in many ways. Here are just a few:

- Your system will save them time because your method is tried-and-true.

- Your system will help organize them. One of the reasons you get clients in the first place is that they are disorganized with regard to their financial planning. They don't know how to proceed.

- Your system helps clients identify their objectives and priorities. Going through the exercise that your system provides will clarify their goals.

- Your system will help clients see where they are going. It will, in effect, chart the course.

- Since clients can now see where they are going, your system will help them accomplish the goals you both have set.

- Your system will help motivate clients to act on the plan. Once everything is spelled out with a definite way to get there, acting becomes a lot easier.

- In the same vein, your system will establish a pattern for clients to follow. In other words, it will become a habit.

- Your system will help you educate clients in the ways of financial planning. Remember, this is a cooperative enterprise; you and your clients work together so that they won't revert to their old ways.

While the following system seems oriented toward a large operation, it can be adapted to a fledgling firm. One person will have to fulfill multiple roles.

Qualifying Clients

Simply put, the best system is the checklist. Like the mathematician, you learned a long time ago that when there's a right way to do something, do it that way all the time. Later you learned that when you must solve a problem of a nonscientific nature, approach it as scientifically as possible to eliminate what won't work. Then make an educated choice among the remaining options and test it. That's how a political pollster works, and it's the basis of market research.

The first thing to find out is whether it will be feasible for a prospective client and you to work together. Can you do enough for each other to warrant entering the type of relationship that will be required until you see the client through to where he or she doesn't need you anymore? Will you be able to save the client enough to merit the fee you must charge, or could his or her money and your time and expertise be better spent? You have a checklist for this, but first a person in your office should qualify the client in the interest of efficiency. Your secretary can serve this role until, and if, you grow your firm.

Since most prospective clients are by referral—as yours should be, too, even if you are just getting started—they will either call your office or come up to you at a seminar or after a speech to inquire about your services. In the latter case, at this point you would ask them to call your office.

One person at your office, perhaps the office manager, takes all those types of calls, asks certain qualifying questions, and states your procedure, which is that you will send pertinent information on yourself, along with an extensive questionnaire for them to complete and bring to the initial meeting (see Appendix A). You then set an appointment date that is about six weeks away to give them enough time to complete the questionnaire. It is a questionnaire for them, but it is a checklist for you. If they don't make an appointment at that time, don't send the questionnaire, because it will intimidate them to terminal procrastination, and they probably weren't serious to begin with. The telephone conversation ends with your guarantee of confidentiality if a meeting is set. In fact, that tone of confidentiality is maintained to the extent that no clients' names should ever be mentioned outside of in-house discussion under penalty of termination. A prospective client who wants a reference from a current or former client must get it on their own.

The analyst, the person responsible for organizing all your cases, will contact the client many times during the pre-presentation period to gather the missing information and documentation from data that accompanied the questionnaire. By the time the actual presentation by the planner rolls around, the client and the analyst will be on near-intimate terms. The analyst organizes each case in a box or attractive file holder like those used by law firms to transport legal-size folders. Refer to the materials and data list in Appendix B. Each line item in that list requires a manila folder.

Besides possessing the obvious organizational skills, an analyst should be an excellent communicator in that he or she is really the person developing the relationship in the beginning and is responsible for the lion's share of sustaining it. Of course, most beginning fee-only planners do this themselves—it's how they learn to ply their trade and develop a system. For me, it was also the biggest incentive to grow rapidly, so that I could afford to hire and train someone to do it for me. A good detail person attuned to your system is invaluable.

Organizing Client Information

As the client information, including insurance policies, wills, and trusts, comes in, the documents are placed in appropriately labeled file folders. The information is then transferred to forms so you do not have to refer continually to all the documents (see Appendix A). The only documents to keep are copies of the tax returns; you don't have a warehouse. Consider scanning all the documents you wish to retain. This will make them more readily available and save storage space in your office. Then all documents and nonessential information are organized within their folders in the box and returned to the client.

The analyst will go through the box with the client, explain the organizational system, and thin out the files so that the client is readily familiar with what is essential. Each form serves two purposes: It covers the necessary points and calculations to ensure proper planning, and it educates the client to the planning process. Keep it simple. You need this information to build your "book" on each client. If clients are confused, it only retards progress. You will go over the book with the client at every meeting. It is an educational tool for you based on the implementation checklist. The biggest mistake planners make at this stage is trying to dazzle clients with reams of multicolored charts and sophisticated computer processes intended to showcase their genius.

The analyst goes over the checklist with the client as far as possible to put together the book before the next meeting. It educates the client, the analyst, and any new associates in the firm. The book is designed to cover all details. It is broken down into sections so that you can cover all the pertinent points in each financial planning area, e.g., estate planning. Within each section there are several points to cover regarding estate planning, e.g., Should you have a will? Is the will you have appropriate? and so on. Then the checklist will offer possible options, e.g., Hire an attorney to prepare a will. This way you can readily update, adjust, and amend. The book allows you to be thorough, and it provides an agenda for each client's case review. After all, the most important part of planning is knowing what to look for. This method ensures that nothing slips through the cracks.

Once the analyst organizes the case and develops the book to the extent possible, the case comes to you for an initial evaluation. It is then distributed to your associates for individual evaluation, and you get together and brainstorm as a group. Do this on a scheduled basis for every case. Over the years, you will have supplemented your skills with the appropriate support skills from people you have hired and trained. This work flow chart is followed as religiously as the checklist. Before your practice matures to this level, take the same steps with your outside specialists and your client's advisors, and if the most minute detail needs clarification, at no stage in your career should you neglect to use their expertise. The client's advisors are already aware of your involvement on his or her behalf. There is no better way to defuse any skepticism on an advisor's part than to request his or her imprimatur on a particular section of specialization. It exhibits your preparedness and versatility as a professional, and it extends to them the respect they deserve. This is the key moment in the success of the plan and your success as a planner—the time when all your technical, organizational, and people skills are showcased for the first time. Be prepared. You don't want any surprises in your presentation to the client.

The First Meeting (Prospective Client Meeting)

Reviewing the Client Questionnaire

At the first meeting with a prospective client, the completed questionnaire becomes a tool for you. The interim between the call and the meeting, during which the questionnaire was to have been completed, has made the client aware of how critical it is to seek help in gaining control of his or her fiscal direction. Now is the time for both of you to consider if you are the one to help. As with any first encounter, the opening moments are psychological and critical. First impressions usually have lasting effects on a relationship. Begin by reiterating your code of confidentiality and explain the function of the questionnaire before reviewing it with the client. Since it will not be completed satisfactorily to draw conclusions at this stage, you can reassure the client that this is nearly always the case and that this first meeting is intended only as a general discussion.

You then let the client's responses in the questionnaire dictate your line of inquiry. Your questions will tell both of you if you should enter a client-planner relationship. If you decide that the person would be attractive as a client, ask questions that will point up the need for your service. Create the want. Ask a series of questions that will introduce better alternatives to the methods that were employed in the past, without being specific. The client's responses will tell you volumes about what your working relationship will be like. Continue probing until you judge that you can work with this client harmoniously and can benefit your practice by adding him or her to your roster.

Compliment clients on things they have done well in the past and criticize only by suggesting alternatives. Things will balance out in your favor because you have all the information. Whoever advised the client in the past did not have all the information, or he or she wouldn't be here. This is where you develop your credibility with prospective clients, and that is best done by exhibiting your efficiency and versatility. Keep it light and conversational, and let the personalities break through. Let them know that their situation isn't the end of the world; it's the beginning, and regardless of what choices they make, your questionnaire at least prompted them to get their documents in order.

After the basic fact-finding portion of the first meeting, get into a general discussion of their goals. Most people can't be specific, but urge them to choose several just to determine realistic parameters. This starts them thinking about direction and process; it reminds them why they came to you and what it is you do. It also reiterates the urgency to make a decision and get on the right track. This comes at the proper time because you are about to quote a fee.

If you are selective in taking on new clients, you will find that an aura of exclusive clientele will turn into a fantastic sales tool. So will the fact that you don't "unbundle" your service. Either do every aspect of a plan or none of it. In fact, the new clients you take on are the ones for which you can do the most. If you are a new planner, you will be tempted to take a piecemeal case. Please don't. It will slow the progress of your comprehensive, fee-only financial planning firm. So right from the outset, as soon as possible, convey this impression to prospects: "If we can take you in . . . , " "If we decide something can be worked out . . . ," and so on. It lets them know you don't need them to be successful, and it only makes them want you more. However, you must watch that fine line between exclusivity and snob appeal.

By now you have taken control of the meeting—not by statements you have made, but by questions you have asked. You have planted seeds of both despair and hope and have let the prospective clients draw their conclusions. You have listened and let them tell you what they want to hear, and you have not committed yourself to anything. They realize the need, and you have created the want if you have used your people skills properly. Their decision now is whether they can afford not to hire you.

Just when clients are thinking about your helping them attain their goals, right after their past deficiencies have been exposed and corrective alternatives have been identified, qualify your availability with something like, "With full cooperation you will be able to maintain the standard of service you require for X dollars per year." Explain how you derived the fee and tell them what full service includes. Make sure they know that you expect them to participate in the process and to guarantee their other advisors' cooperation—that is part of the agreement.

After I have quoted them the fee and explained how I determined it, I usually truthfully add, "I wouldn't have quoted you the fee if I didn't think I could earn it." Tell them they should think about it and let you know whether they wish to proceed. Give them a written copy of the quote and your Form ADV (Appendix E).

Tell them you will need a reply within five business days. There should be no pressure from you to close the sale. Because this is the beginning of a long-term relationship, you want them to make the decision without perceived pressure, taking action only after due deliberation. Even as a beginner, you must imply your exclusivity. Begin thinking this way from the first day you start your business and place a premium on your services.

You are extending them a loose leash, and now you will close the meeting by drawing it in a bit. Tell them that since there will be much more information to be gathered for the next meeting should they decide to proceed, they are more than welcome to leave what they brought for today with you so you can have it organized in advance. If they decline to proceed, you will be more than happy to return the materials. That's an attractive offer, and if they accept it, they are semicommitted. Tell them that upon receiving their call of confirmation to proceed, your office manager will send an invoice requesting a deposit of 50% of the total fee payable on receipt (see sample confirmation letter and invoice in Appendix B). Explain that you require 50% because more than half of the work required on the client's case will be completed by the conclusion of your next meeting a month hence. The initial exploratory meeting concludes after approximately one hour at no cost to the prospective client.

If the client does not call within the five days, I do not call to follow up. I prefer to lose them now rather than after I have invested a great deal in them.

Dealing with Rejection

Let's pause for a moment to dwell on rejection and the effects it can have, especially at the outset of a career. It's going to happen no matter how well you present your services, but it will occur less frequently as you gain experience. What you can control is the rate of frequency.

Learn to scrutinize each presentation and, like a true salesperson, determine what did or didn't work in each case. Most of the time, when you talked too much instead of listening, you lost out. You didn't wait for the prospective client to tell you what he or she wanted to say; instead, you said what you wanted to say. I had a former partner who used to take an hour and a half just to say hello. Clients would complain because of this lack of consideration. Even when you don't overstate your case and you do respond correctly, you will lose some clients simply because what you offer, while it may be best for some people, isn't right for them. In that case, the rejection is best for you, too.

The Second Meeting (First Presentation Meeting)

From the outset of the second meeting, your first meeting together as client and planner, insist on extensive note taking and record keeping on both your parts. Beyond being the essence of organization, the notes and records become a summary of what you have done and where you are going. Memory never serves in the simplest of tasks and would hardly serve in even the smallest phase of financial planning. From your notes emerge memos to batch and send out weekly as reminders to the client of who is responsible for what at what time, especially through the implementation stage. Some have the assistant take notes while the meeting is conducted. Others are interactive and take notes that are shown on a computer monitor so that the client can see them as they are made. This second choice is my preference. I explain that this method prevents misunderstandings. If I put the wrong information in the note, the client can immediately correct it. At the end of the meeting, I print the meeting notes for the client to take.

The first hour of the second meeting involves the client and analyst. The focus is on completing all fact-finding and verification. The analyst gives the client the box and goes over the organizational flow. It's also the time to cement the working arrangement between the two, because hereafter all updates, changes, and modifications in the portfolio will be channeled through the analyst to and from the planner, except for meetings, which are scheduled at regular intervals as required.

The last hour of the second meeting involves the client (both spouses), and you. By allowing the analyst to set the table, you have given him or her the credibility needed to get the client's full disclosure and cooperation. Now is the time to show the results of the combined efforts of the past weeks, in skeleton form. Briefly recap the salient points of your evaluation to let them know you have done your homework and to command their full attention, for now the planning process has begun.

Income Planning

In developing a plan, the most important section to cover first is income planning. It is the potential source of wealth for most of your clients, and generally the one of most concern to them. They may be concerned from the perspective of either cash flow or income taxes, and with both in mind you must put together a retirement income forecast. It's important to let clients understand the tax implications of what they are currently doing with their cash flow and what those implications will be with what you suggest.

It's difficult to forecast five months into the future, let alone five years, but you need to show some foresight and start your clients thinking. It's also critical to get them thinking about the management of their personal cash flow and what their cash flow needs are going to be over the next 12 months. This is not a budget, but a forecast. You are not interested in history. You want to know what they plan to do this year because it is the basis on which they set goals. They must take into account possible retirement, disability, or death, and the effects each would have on their cash flow, as things exist and as adjustments are made. Sample worksheets for cash flow and disability planning are included in Appendix C.

With that, set about to establish realistic goals. Most clients tend to be unrealistic about how much cash they have and fail to account for things that may interrupt their cash flow. You must force them to focus on all the worst scenarios because you have to account for everything. Help them set up a cash flow worksheet to cover the 12-month period with all the necessary provisions—retirement, insurance, children's education, implementation of your recommendations, taxes, and so on—subject to periodic review. If they are within 10% a month deviation, don't worry. Above that and you have to improve on their cash flow management, or their goals are unrealistic. Clients' goals will be redefined continually throughout the first years as they learn the process. They are forced to employ "suffocating logic" to see the reality of their positions and make whatever compromises may be necessary to achieve financial independence. Keep in mind that if you told clients they would need to make these concessions rather than showing them, they would likely have cut back by firing you.

Retirement and Investment Planning

The next area to attend to is retirement planning, because it is the real reason the client is investing. It may require some excess capital and will be predicated largely upon what can be saved in general as well as in taxes through the utilization of tools over the planning period.

Following in order and concluding the second client-planner meeting are education planning, investment planning, and cash flow projections. Samples of these worksheets are included in Appendix C. Today, of course, there are a myriad of financial planning software packages you may wish to explore. Do not make your decision regarding this software based on cost. Most successful planners eventually create their own spreadsheets. Your clients need you to dissect their financial situations and deal with each of these areas individually. However, more than that, you must help them pull everything together in a coordinated fashion. Most planners fail to do this realistically because of their product orientation and disdain for the process. For me, seeing it all come together is a challenge fulfilled. That is why it is wise to attend to details in the checklists, reducing the margin for error and leaving nothing to chance. The sooner clients see the process begin to work, to see the after-tax rate of return on their investments increase sufficiently to make their goals attainable, the faster the dominoes fall, and the plan matures. A good system is designed to make clients see it in action.

It is obvious from the checklists that you require extensive detail for every investment analysis. Most people don't know how well or poorly they are performing, or even what their after-tax rate of return is; yet this is the most important percentage to understand because it is the amount of money they get to keep. If you can demonstrate the effects of your recommendations, clients will be more willing to do what you want them to do in order to reach their goals. There are only a few routes to those goals: saving more money per year, reducing expenses, or increasing the rate of return on investments. When clients can gauge your proficiency in forecasting during your periodic reviews, they will be increasingly inclined to authorize the implementation required to maintain the plan in action. Do not get carried away with the investment section of the plan. By now, as you guessed, there should be a checklist for these meetings as well. Consider creating a schedule of areas to be reviewed for each quarterly meeting.

Remember, you are a comprehensive planner, and investing is only a part of the plan. It is no more important than estate planning, education planning, or retirement planning. If you want to be an investment planner, then do that rather than disguise yourself as a comprehensive financial planner. Be wary of the fee-only planners who focus on this aspect of the plan. Often, they create as large a conflict of interest as the commission-oriented planner because they are attempting to gain more investments to manage so they can charge a higher fee.

By the conclusion of the second meeting you have touched on every aspect of the client's financial life in search of every bit of information you need to establish a course of action. You have helped set up a cash flow worksheet to establish realistic goals, and you have started the client thinking in the right direction. You have organized the data and presented it in book form, and you have begun to plot a course for the future. The client is sent home for a month to digest what transpired. Your clients will have plenty of homework because they know you expect them to become as efficient as you have been.

The Third Meeting

The second meeting emphasized analysis, evaluation, and action, all predicated on order. The third meeting, already scheduled for the following month, will attend to estate planning, insurance needs, and business interests, so the client has much more to prepare. The client will discuss your recommendations with his or her advisors and, more importantly, with his or her spouse—

the essential partner in this. Remember that a spouse can have more influence on your client than even the most trusted advisor. Client and spouse must work together if they are to change their way of doing business and become part of the process. Generally speaking, it is a danger signal when only one spouse attends all the meetings.

The early stages of the third meeting revolve around questions that have cropped up since the last meeting. This is a critical time for both of you because the client needs reassurance, and you need to gauge the level of response to your recommendations. You must judge his or her aptitude and attitude to determine your pace. You will know the client's level of retention from the line of questioning, and how the client feels about what lies ahead by the level of preparation for this third meeting. You must strike the psychological chord that will elicit maximum response from the client in the cooperative venture you have entered. It's different for everyone, but it's usually found in the person's goals. What does he or she want to accomplish the most, and how realistically achievable is it? If it's a practical ideal, show the client how to pursue it within the framework of the plan. If it's totally impractical, show what is readily attainable with his or her resources and offer viable alternatives to the ideal. You have to agree on a goal because the next meeting is when decisions are made.

The Fourth Meeting

Thirty days hence is the time for the fourth meeting. By now you have probably refined your recommendations with the requisite specialists, your professionals, and the client's advisors, within their individual fields. Whenever possible all the meetings, including this one, will be held in your office with the client (both spouses) and possibly certain of the client's advisors. The location adds to your control, as does your knowledge that the advisors may know more about their fields of specialization than you do, but none of them knows nearly as much as you do about all the related fields of financial planning. You must show them this, not tell them, and you do so through preparation, experience, and objectivity.

Become the advocate, not so much of your recommendations per se, but of the client. You are the only one there with the ability to coordinate them all into a cohesive flow and direct them to the fulfillment of the client's goals. None of the other specialists has had all of the pieces of the puzzle. They find, as you proceed, that the process does not exclude them; it involves them. They cannot question your objectives and remain credible with their client. Very rarely is consensus approval not obtained.

Now, about 90 days after the 50% deposit is invoiced, another payment falls due and is billed.

Implementation

After the decisions are made, a priority schedule is set and implementation begins. This will involve as many meetings and phone conversations with specialists or providers as necessary to get the plan in action as quickly as possible. The implementation checklist in Appendix D can help you organize and carry out your planning recommendations. Expediency is essential. It sets the tone and pace that must be maintained, and it establishes a working relationship with the advisors. Now, for the first time, the plan takes on worth.

Implementation is by far the most important aspect of financial planning. Without total implementation, your clients are no better off for having worked with you than they were before they came to you. In fact, they may be worse off. Before they began working with you, they might not have realized how bad their situation was. Now they know, but they don't know what to do about it, or they are overwhelmed with what has to be done.

No other area better distinguishes the advantages of being a fee-only planner than implementation. No other area in financial planning offers the opportunity to distinguish between financial services and financial planning more clearly than this one does. Yet this is the area where the greatest confusion exists in the minds of other planners, clients, and the media.

Several years ago, a respected research firm conducted a survey to determine the public's perception of implementation. The survey found that the public equated the term "implementation" with placement of a product. In other words, implementation equalled sales.

If that were true, then implementation as viewed by fee-only financial planners would be an incomplete process. Such items as updating a will or trust, negotiating a business agreement, cash flow planning, and the preparation of a balance sheet would not be implementation and could be left uncompleted. However, they are as important a part of the implementation process as investing in a mutual fund or a limited partnership.

If a planner falls into the trap of focusing on investing, his or her clients will evaluate service based on the current year's investment return. This would be deadly. One bad investment year would cause the clients to run to an investment advisor, because that's how they would view the planner. The client would lose both total financial planning and an understanding of what financial planning is.

The fee-only planner is the only financial planning professional who can provide complete implementation. He or she is the only one who can truly co-ordinate and manage the integrated efforts of all the specialists, such as the lawyer with the will and the insurance agent with the life insurance package.

However, some fee-only planners do not understand the concept of complete implementation. They fall into the trap of dealing only with the areas they feel comfortable in, such as investing. Investment planning is only part of the financial planning process. Because of this misunderstanding, new planners worry about putting deals together for their clients. They are concerned about not being able to find no-load investments. They worry if they can't take an entire offering rather than just a portion.

Implementation is more than investments. It's everything you do to help your clients achieve the goals you have set together.

Common Implementation Errors

Even experienced financial planners, including fee-only practitioners, make mistakes when it comes to implementation. Some of the more common errors are as follows:

- Lack of coordination among the components of the portfolio of investments, insurance programs, real estate holdings, and tax strategies.

- Too much emphasis on tax shelters (not since the Tax Reform Act of 1986).

- No clear objectives for implementation.

- Not enough effort given to estate planning.

- Trying to be an expert in areas in which the planner is not competent.

Management Review

Management maintenance and review meetings follow the completion of the initial stages of implementation, generally on a quarterly basis. These are supplemented in your office by in-house monthly reviews and status reports done by the analyst and shared with the team (see Appendix D). The recommendations are given to the client at each meeting with applicable information for him or her. The purposes of these quarterly reviews vary with each client, although there is a formal agenda. A doctor might call them routine checkups, and the analogy is appropriate because you want to take your clients' temperatures, so to speak. Are they apprehensive about anything? Confused? Do they still care? What changes have gone on in their lives? Are they still committed to their goals? What's the latest news in the field? Are their goals still consistent with what you are planning to achieve?

There is never a lack of things to talk about, for you have entered into a relationship that must grow to endure. You are now familiar with the client's advisors and have dealt with them professionally. The client, in turn, is now familiar with your analyst and how your office functions. You can nip any problems in the bud so they won't fester and infect the plan or the relationship. Appropriate adjustments in the plan are authorized at these meetings and scheduled for implementation.

One hundred and eighty days after the initial deposit, the final payment of the total fee is invoiced and the client has paid in full for the year.

At the conclusion of the first year, you start all over. I have developed a review schedule to make certain every item is covered. This schedule eliminates the bottleneck of having to prepare a complete new review as we used to do. Focus on certain aspects of the plan for each quarterly meeting. This will enable the client to anticipate the agenda and value the quarterly scheduled meeting. For example, our schedule includes tax and retirement planning in the first quarter, with dependents, investments, and investing covered in the second quarter. The third quarter focuses on non-equity investments, life and health insurance including long-term care, disability, and so on. The fourth quarter deals with estate planning, property and casualty insurance, and tax planning again. Remember, financial planning is a process and works best on an ongoing, long-term basis.

Alternatives: In Style, but Not in Substance

The password to your system is action. You want to establish the pace, set the tone, and move ahead. You don't want to have to rekindle the flame continually. Once you get past the tedium, the rest is exciting. That's why you made it your career, and that's also why the key person in the early part of the process is the analyst. Your analyst's skills complement your own strengths so that you are free to plan and coordinate. Remember, in the beginning you are the analyst. Since you can't do it all, spend your time where you can do the most good, where you can make your services the best available.

My style might not be appropriate for another practitioner, but it is best for me. Sooner or later every successful full-service plan will, by necessity, include nearly every substantive element found in mine. The techniques employed to assimilate the information and motivate the clients can be unique to each fee-only planner as long as they are successful in creating the want.

Developing Client Relationships

More and more people today are looking for your services as a fee-only planner, but to whom should you direct your marketing efforts? Pursue those groups with whom you are most credible and compatible.

All beginning fee-only planners are torn between going after the first big client to establish themselves and taking on a couple of smaller clients to refine their systems. However, you don't yet have sufficient credibility to land the big client. The drawback to having smaller clients is that you may not generate enough income from them unless you follow the recommendations in chapters 5 and 6 for preparing your own business plan and setting up a system.

Targeting Your Market

The answer is to determine which markets offer you the most ready access and to which ones you best relate. This is a personal decision that will differ for each planner. What's certain is that the best clients to pursue are those from a background similar to yours. If you went to an Ivy League college, approach others with that background. Or, if you were an officer in the armed forces, other former officers are naturals to approach. You get the idea. Find individuals or groups you can naturally relate to and seek business from them. If you do not feel you have a definitive group from your background, you will need to research the group you are targeting. Find books written about the group. Subscribe to magazines that are group-related (i.e., association magazines). You need to learn about members' lifestyles, problems, interests, and so on. Also accept the fact you may gravitate to a diverse group. In my own case, my client mix has continued to change over the years. My earliest clients were dentists and now I have very few dentists.

A stockbroker making the transition to fee-only planning should have a natural affinity for corporate officers and business owners, especially those who might have been clients in the past. If the stockbroker's clients were happy with him or her as a stockbroker, they should continue to trust his or her judgment now.

Professionals need most of all to trust their planner's judgment. These people are highly intelligent in their own spheres, but they are often woefully uninformed about financial planning. Who better to trust than a fellow professional? Therefore, if you are a former accountant or attorney turned fee-only planner, your natural markets are former colleagues, physicians, dentists, engineers, real estate agents, and architects, to name just a few. Because they are so well informed in their own fields, they insist on dealing professionally with those who are equally informed in their own.

The former insurance agent turned fee-only planner probably has the best deal of all. He or she has ready access to all of the groups mentioned so far and also others such as two-income families, widows, and people with large inheritances. Frequency of contact has a bearing on relative credibility, and some people simply have reason to contact their insurance agents more frequently for service than they do their brokers, accountants or attorneys. Once again, compatibility, credibility, and accessibility are key.

Even more fun to work with because they are entrepreneurial are business owners. They can plan around their businesses, and they are used to being decisive. They can both order and delegate. Business owners are fascinating to work with because you can use their business and its employees to design a plan for their personal gain. They generally respond very well to the education you provide. I see lots of challenges, lots of diverse goals, many unique individuals, and an opportunity for the fee-only planner to use a full range of skills.

The rest of the corporate market is more restricted. Smaller-salaried employees will naturally have to compromise with the planner building around the company fringe benefit package. You will normally be able to help them with cash flow, budgeting, college for the kids, or life insurance.

Higher-up corporate executives should build around the company package too, but they will need and want much more because they have grown used to a certain lifestyle. That lifestyle is, however, subject to the vagaries of economics, particularly inflation. These individuals will have tax and investment problems and might need a 401(k) program. They are concerned about sending their kids to the best colleges. Estate planning is a priority with them.

Chief executive officers usually like to involve themselves in the implementation program, but since they delegate authority without even thinking about it, you will probably find yourself dealing with their aides and assistants in implementing the plan. These CEOs are, however, used to making important decisions about their individual well-being and will be familiar with more of the material you present than any other group.

Two-income families are usually the most difficult to plan for because they never have as many assets as they think they have and as a result are usually attracted to the quick fix. They tend to get in over their heads. They spend both of their incomes instead of saving. They generally are tentative and unsophisticated, need cash flow management, and, once planned for, are the least likely to follow through on implementation.

Another difficult group are widows who are left very well off and other individuals who inherit large sums of money. Whatever the planner proposes is not good enough because it is inevitably different from what the person who accumulated the fortune would have done. These people rarely respond to your suggestions because you are dealing with ghosts who have become legends.

Clients can also be classified by income brackets. This method puts things in perspective for both the client and the planner.

People with incomes of $50,000 or less could do their own financial planning. As discussed earlier, this could be your beginning market. They can't indulge their wants realistically because they have to satisfy their needs first. They should, however, learn the financial planning process.

They can do this by forming financial planning clubs, similar to investment clubs. The club can then hire a fee-only planner to teach members how to do a financial plan. The planner's duties would include outlining goals, coordinating club activities, creating the format for the club, providing counsel, aiding in implementation, and monitoring the progress of implementation. The planner is, in effect, the club's director, and the club is the client. To the best of my knowledge, this has never been attempted, but it seems like a good way to help the greatest number of people who really need the discipline that financial planning affords. It could be the wave of the future.

Individuals in the $50,000 to $100,000 bracket are similar in many ways to the two-earner families discussed earlier. They are primarily concerned with developing their lifestyles.

Above $100,000 in income is the level you should be looking at. Not only are these people amenable to your suggestions and help, but they are normally ready to work with you, especially if you want to do some new things.

Encouraging Client Involvement

One of the functions of your system is to set the tone for the client-planner relationship. The system must be designed to provoke action, to force decisions with little or no wasted motion. When clients sit across the desk from you for the first time, they already know they need your service. What they probably don't know is what all those services include and how badly they really need them. Don't try to sell your service; impress your clients with how you operate. Remember, though, your skill as a planner will go largely untested if you can't create the want from among the people who already know they have the need for your services.

You must be both professional and personable. Don't waste their time, but you must take time to assure clients of the value of the relationship. It really does matter if you both like each other. Successful financial plans are very personal things, so an atmosphere of comfortable cooperation is essential. This is most readily achieved by working through the framework of your system. The fact that you are fully prepared puts prospective clients at ease and allows you to control the direction of the interview. Again, there's that word "control." It's vital that you have it and use it.

However, control is not enough if you don't have outstanding people skills. If you stray from your system, you will lose control, and your relationships with your clients will break down. By staying organized and following a well-thought-out pattern of questioning, you can catalog impressions and reactions that are unique to each individual. If you can recall them later, you will be able to strengthen the bonds with your clients.

As indicated before, next to the planner, the client has to be the plan's most active participant. However, getting a client to participate actively is often a difficult matter. Key to cooperation is the level of communication established between the client and your analyst. Remember, except for meetings, all communication pertaining to the plan will take place between the client (or the client's advisors) and the analyst. In the beginning, remember, this may be you. The analyst makes a living collecting, documenting, and organizing financial data. The client does not; yet for the first six weeks of this new relationship, that is precisely what he or she will have to do.

The sooner the research and documentation are complete, the sooner the client can leave things in the hands of your professional team. The analyst then has to expedite the process. This will require people skills of the highest order. The analyst will need to communicate with advisors who may be reluctant to help out because they don't trust you yet.

Since, in my experience, most clients won't truly begin to come to grips with the really hard goals of the plan for three to five years, it's important to begin with cash flow and projections. Once they see what they are up against and how you have laid it all out for them, then you really have them as clients for life. All of their psychological resistance to financial planning will have evaporated.

Clients want to have confidence in you, to trust you. You must look for ways to reinforce that trust. The most important tool you have to inspire this trust is the code of confidentiality you must maintain as a professional. The information left in your charge is far too personal to be even broadly hinted at outside the office.

However, while you're gathering the information you need, nothing is out of bounds. You must constantly ask questions as you go over the checklists and questionnaire. How do they feel about such and such? Have they ever considered this or that? These inquiries can be about investment alternatives, insurance, goals, or any other financial matter. The point is, if you want to know something, don't neglect to ask. It's important to retain your curiosity and imagination as you evaluate alternatives and the client's response to them. The planner's curiosity inspires the client and adds to the trusting relationship that you are working to cement.

Obviously, all the participants' responsibilities are carefully delineated in the simplest possible terms. With everyone—especially you—acting professionally, problems should be minimized. Remember, until clients are presented with their books, they usually have some apprehension about the entire process. Moreover, unless their advisors have worked with fee-only planners before, they, too, will probably be skeptical.

You need to remain totally professional, enabling your position as client advocate to obviate any need to defend your services. At this point you might try to redirect the thinking of professionals who react that way.

One of the items set out in Appendix E is a letter of authorization that can be used by any firm or fee-only planner. Also included are samples of written correspondence from my office to clients and their advisors that I have used in the initial stages of the planning process. You can use them to develop that all-important client relationship that will be the cornerstone of your success in this business.

Establishing and Maintaining a Client Relationship

From the first meeting, you are striving to build a client relationship that will grow. Even though you want to use your analyst to handle the data gathering and analysis, don't become too distant from the client. Some firms seem to imply, "I'm very important and busy; talk to my assistant." Do not confuse the setting up of a system to make your practice run smoothly with starting a bureaucracy where you are protected by layers of employees. You need to be available while still directing the client to work with the analyst.

Establishing a relationship with the client's advisors is an important part of building client relationships. Do not try to be a one-stop shopping center that provides legal, accounting, and other services. The client's present advisors may have well-established relationships, even friendships with them. When you show the client's advisor that you are competent and professional, the advisor will respect you; this in turn enhances your credibility and stature with the client. Your goal is to build a personal, company, and professional image that says exactly what you want to say. As your client sees these different aspects of you, your relationship is strengthened. You will be evaluated on how you talk about your family and your personal beliefs.

Does your office environment support what you are saying with family pictures, plaques from groups you support, and so forth? Personal values are important as a fee-only financial planner. If your office is neat and well organized, then clients will believe that you can organize their financial world. Everything within your office and leaving your office, from stationery, brochures, and letters to office decor and staff should reflect the image you want.

Handling telephone calls is a key area. Train the person answering the phone to reflect the image you want. If that person does not know telephone etiquette or is discourteous or bored, you will lose significant business and not even know it.

Your education enhances your professional image. As your clients enter your office, they should be able to view the framed degrees you've earned, awards you've received, articles you've written, and so on. Seeing these outward symbols of your success confirms their confidence in your abilities. The clients can see they made the right choice in hiring you.

Having talked about the importance of image, there is one caveat. Do not attempt to project an image that is not truly you. You cannot act the part all the time. The moment you slip back into your true self, you have destroyed your credibility and trust with clients. This is not to say that you cannot change your own image if you really want to improve, but it will take time, perhaps outside consultants, and practice to change your accent, speech patterns, gestures, and other characteristics to conform to your desired client group's image. If you believe that this self-improvement is necessary for your practice, do not undertake this project without consultation with your spouse and your own advisors.

How to Market and Survive in a Fee-Only Practice

No matter what the business, marketing is usually the key to success. Most new millionaires in our society today owe their status to how well they marketed their products and services. They either marketed something common uncommonly well or they marketed something uncommon to a common audience.

Be certain you don't jump on the bandwagon of the idea of the month. Many years ago we taught planners to consider the whole client, including the client's personal needs. Jim Schwartz, one of the three founders of NAPFA, introduced the concept of holistic treatment of a client through his book, *Enough* (New York: MasterMedia Limited, 1995). It seems today there is an overabundance of touchy-feely approaches. The investment success of recent markets has led many planners to focus on investing instead of comprehensive planning. Stay on point. We are fee-only, comprehensive financial planners.

Marketing a Concept

Successful marketing, for the most part, involves finding something unique or unusual to attract the attention of the public. To market and survive as a fee-only planner in this day and age, it is necessary to market the concept of fee-only planning itself.

In marketing the fee-only concept, the planner should use a positive approach. Instead of demeaning other types of planners, inform the public that there are different types of planners and present exactly who and what you are. Some will still prefer one of the other types, but it is not your mission to convert the world. Your job is to work with informed clients with whom you can build a long-lasting and worthwhile relationship. You might consider developing some guidelines for prospects to follow in evaluating and selecting a planner. A sample is included in Appendix E.

Costs

Teach consumers to have each type of planner fully disclose all costs associated with the planning to be done. Perhaps at this point the disclosure form developed by NAPFA (the National Association of Personal Financial Advisors; www.napfa.com) would be helpful to you and the consumer. Remember, your competitors will be depicting you as being more expensive, so you must understand the cost differences and demonstrate how your services will be less expensive than those of your non-fee-only competitors.

Objectivity

Another unique advantage that you can exploit in your marketing is the fee-only planner's objectivity. The public perceives someone who works strictly for a fee as more objective than someone who sells a product.

Point out that other professionals such as attorneys and CPAs operate on a fee-for-services basis and that you do, too. Also promote yourself in this manner to companies and individuals that provide products and services your client will need, such as life insurance. When they understand you are not selling a competitive product and that you don't expect to participate in their commissions, these providers may refer clients to you. They realize that if you recommend their products to your clients, they make the same money in less time. Finally, the other professional advisors you try to compare yourself to may be more willing to refer clients to you because they perceive no conflict of interest.

When you contact your client's other advisors, take the time to educate them on how your objectivity will benefit them. If they offer a good service, you will be willing to refer other clients to these advisors because you are looking out for your clients' best interests. Don't expect to do this only once. Remind them until they are educated on the advantages of fee-only planning.

If you encounter errors in the work that a client's advisors have performed, you can demonstrate your objectivity while being sensitive to egos. Point out the error to the advisor. He or she should offer to correct it. You should think through this scenario ahead of time so you will know how you want to handle it with both the advisor and your client.

If another advisor continues to do poor or inaccurate work, you will have to inform the client. Do this in such a manner that the client makes the decision to fire the advisor, not you. If the client refused to fire that advisor, what would your response be?

Competence

However, no matter how much less you charge for your service or how objective you are, nothing will sell you to the public more than your competence at financial planning. It's important to study as much as you can as often as you can. The more you know, the more you can help your clients. By word of mouth alone, you will end up with more clients than you can handle.

Again, in your interactions with your client's advisors, it is imperative that your actions stress your competence. If you don't know the answer, say so and get back to them after you have researched the answer. Don't overlook the possibility of attracting these advisors as your clients. Ask them if they have personal financial plans that are comprehensive. If these advisors observe you at work in preparing a plan, either their client's or their own, they will be more inclined to make referrals to you.

Implementation

When presenting your case, don't forget about your superiority as an implementer. Tell prospects that because of your unique position as a nonsalesperson, you can be approached by everyone selling a product or service. As a result, you can choose from a greater selection to the benefit of your client.

Point out this benefit to your client's advisors also. If they offer a quality product at a reasonable cost, they can count on you to refer clients to them.

If you can market the advantages of your fee-only practice, you should be successful at reaching your target audience. Mostly, though, you are marketing yourself.

Marketing Yourself—Some Tried-and-True Methods

Make sure that your very first client is well served and satisfied, and you will be recommended to others. Be sure that the client's other advisors see the advantages of your fee-only practice for their client. After they work with you and learn that you are competent and trustworthy, you will get referrals from those advisors.

How do you find the first or the ninety-first client? You employ three time-tested methods: Project a professional image, go to the client, and write and be written about.

Project a Professional Image

As a fee-only planner, you will inhabit the world of financial services. To attract clients, you will have to project a certain image. Even the name of your company will be important. I have always felt it was important to have my name in the name of the company. Many, however, tell you to create some incredibly impressive, nonpersonal name. Often, that advice is to create an entity identification rather than a personal one. I believe we are in *personal* financial planning. It is also reassuring to the prospective clients to realize they are dealing with the owner.

First of all, that image has to be a *conservative* one. People are more willing to entrust their money and their financial plans to a conservatively appointed person in a conservative office in a conservative part of town. The client would rather see a limousine than a Ferrari out front. This image extends to your staff and support personnel, even your office and its furnishings. The conservative image projects the idea that care is being exercised in the disposition of a client's assets. Your clients may be flashier than you are, but they want you to be conservative.

Your image also has to be *professional*. This connotes respect and consideration. This means adhering to scheduled appointments, being fully organized and prepared, and acknowledging the efforts of others.

Learn to operate *efficiently*. Perfect your system. That's how you lock in your clients and develop their trust. Since most of your early clients will come through referrals from your original clients, your system becomes both a marketing and a planning tool.

The most crucial aspect of the image you project is that it must radiate *success*. Your first office accommodated your system then; so should your current facilities accommodate your system as it is refined with your expanded practice. Avoid garishness and unnecessary frills. Have no unused space or empty desks. Create an environment conducive to your profession.

Go to the Client

Once you hone your professional image, you can become involved in activities that will give you visibility in different client markets. Every planner should try at least one of these strategies.

1. *Public speaking appearances.* They are excellent for honing valuable speaking skills. Nowadays, financial planning is a hot topic, so you should have plenty of opportunities to speak—if you actively solicit them.

   It's vital that you research your audience, speak in generalities to inspire questions, and emphasize the financial planning process of coordinating all the interrelated aspects toward reaching a common goal. Be sure that the individual who introduces you to the group is a credible person and that he or she is provided with an accurate resume of your experience beforehand. But don't be a salesperson here. If your talk is interesting and you answer questions with a lot of good information, someone in the audience will contact you.

   Look for opportunities to volunteer your expertise to your church or synagogue. You can hold seminars for related topics or specific needs, (e.g., widows). Offer to do free financial reviews for those in need. No one may use you, but your name is in the weekly bulletin. Local groups like the Rotary are always looking for speakers. Contact them.

2. *Teaching.* Whether as a guest lecturer at a high school or community college or as an adjunct professor at a nearby university, teaching is an excellent way to establish your credibility in the community. You also can teach before church groups, investment clubs, and social organizations such as the local YMCA or Kiwanis.

3. *Seminars.* Either as a participant or as the sole leader, these are superb for reaching a targeted audience. In the beginning, no group is too small. If you can address the weekly investment club in your neighborhood, for example, do it.

   The more seminars you do, the more people will know about you and the better you will be able to tell your story. I still do seminars because they allow me total control. I can select the audience I wish to attract, provide the agenda, and engage the appropriate support specialists from among my associates. My practice has grown in concentric circles outward from its core as I have refined my system. Speaking and teaching are excellent ways to set up and prepare for seminars that will attract clients.

4. *Community involvement.* Join the chamber of commerce, philanthropic organizations, church groups, and other organizations, and take an active role in these groups. Here is where you can develop centers of influence. Networking in this manner will help your name recognition. Ultimately, you will receive some referrals.

5. *Professional association involvement.* Be sure you serve in an active role in your local associations. You will come to know leaders in the community because of your service to the association. While representing the association, you will be given press opportunities.

I like these marketing techniques because they take me to where the clients are, and then they come to me. I create the want at their pace, coming across not as a salesperson, but as a professional. When I got enough experience from referrals to realize that I wanted to specialize in professionals, I targeted my efforts toward them, but initially I spoke to anyone who could get three or more people to listen to me.

Write and Be Written About

Let's not forget the written word. Many fee-only planners have columns in local newspapers, which give them excellent exposure. Have no fear about talking to local editors about a column; they may welcome one. Do not worry if you're not a great writer—the copy editors will clean up your articles. The one thing they will insist on is that you meet your deadlines for the column. Make a list of the publications with which you would like to work. Get the names of the appropriate contacts, usually from the publications' mastheads or from the local library.

Offer yourself as a source to financial columnists and money-oriented magazines. If you are quotable, if you provide them with good information, and if you are not selling anything, you will be quoted time and again. Few things will impress a potential client more than picking up a nice article in which you are quoted. If that copy is strategically placed in your reception area, the client will come into your office with a built-in respect for your knowledge.

Do not be afraid to start small. Cultivate a credible relationship with your local media outlets. One way to begin is by writing letters to the editor of the local newspaper with appropriate commentary on topical financial matters. You can promote your expertise to publications by suggesting ideas for stories and sending out press releases. Show how your article ideas will interest their readers. Prepare a press kit you can send out as well as a public relations brochure for potential clients. Always include your curriculum vitae, but keep it to one page. You can also volunteer to assist in researching upcoming features for print or broadcast media. Make yourself known to them as an expert on personal finance. Again, your hobby association, church, synagogue, or other organization may have newsletters where you can contribute.

When journalists begin to contact you, always ask about their deadlines. Take their calls immediately, or as soon as possible return the call. A journalist usually has a short time in which to produce an article and will be grateful for your prompt response. However, be sure to develop a thick skin. You may spend hours providing material for a story only to find out you are not quoted at all. It happens to all of us sooner or later. Be thankful when you are quoted, because you won't see your name in every article you helped on.

Once you do become known—once you are written about, or write your own copy, or do a radio or television show of your own—you become credible. Soon it will begin to pay off, and you may even have the enjoyment of being a local celebrity.

A more common alternative for the low-key fee-only practitioner is to hire someone to attract clients and contribute to the planning process. Less training is required, the person can more objectively select quality over quantity, and loyalty is higher. He or she can serve as an intern or as a full-time contributing staff member, and the planner fills two voids at one price.

Tried and Untrue Methods

The rest of the available marketing tools transcend marketing itself for our purposes and become merchandising. Merchandising + marketing = product promotion. I don't like merchandising in financial planning for several reasons.

First, it doesn't work for the fee-only planner. It's prohibitively expensive, and it must be sustained for long periods to have any effect. It's never cost-effective. We're trying to sell a process. Marketing can tell us how to proceed, but the effective advertisement communicating our message is light-years away.

The tried-and-true methods work for the fee-only planner. If they don't, something is wrong that advertising won't cure. Why should I pay thousands of dollars for media coverage when I can get better, more credible coverage for free with a little initiative?

Second, there's no receptive audience for our process in most advertising outlets. The big brokerage houses and insurance companies advertise financial planning to sell securities and policies. It gets them in the door. If the representatives actually sat down to talk process objectively, they would make about four sales a year.

Third, if there were a way, and if enough fee-only planners wanted to invest the required fortune to compete with the conglomerates in an advertising war, and if there were a common audience—none of which is the case—more clients would be lost than gained. Why? Because we would have cheapened our services to the level of our off-the-rack competitors in the eyes of the exclusive cadre of individuals of interest to us.

Advertising in financial planning to this point has primarily been the tactic used by fee-based and commissioned planners to disguise their packages. It's been based on millions of dollars' worth of market research and development, and it's effective to get them in the door. We fee-only professionals should dissociate ourselves from such tactics and develop from within. The process we offer will emerge predominant if we continue to make the distinction between product indoctrination and a genuine interest in client welfare. Given a qualified and attentive audience, grouped through carefully targeted market research, the advantages of the tactics we profess are irrefutable. The farther we stay from commercializing the process, the sooner we will distance ourselves from the competition.

Marketing oneself through the mail can be effective when addresses are carefully researched and targeted, but this strategy smacks of fee-based and commission orientation. The shotgun approach is worthless and expensive. Just consider your own mail. Most of the people who respond to mass mailings are the ones you wish would not, so the outgoing mail from my office is private and pertinent. Some fee-only planners put out newsletters to their clients and referrals, but I'm in touch with mine so often that I wouldn't have anything to add. Besides, I don't feel a client likes to be thought of as part of a category but rather as an individual, and in order to mail there has to be a mailing list, which would risk exposure of my client roster.

As a marketing tool, once researched, targeted, and properly prepared (at much expense), a mass mailing may have more than marginal potential, but I'm unaware of any appreciable long-term value to fee-only planners. Of course, I'm also unaware of the proper attention having been given to doing it right. That should be an integral part of the "first great survey" you commission.

A Commonsense Method

Help each other. There's more than enough business to go around, and will be long after you retire, so learn to share potential clients and specialists. If you plan for jockeys and psychiatrists in New York, you might refer artists and models to a colleague on Long Island.

What goes around comes around. By marketing the whole concept of fee-only planning, you will ultimately benefit. Be active in NAPFA, and take advantage of its provisions. Market yourself every day in everything you do. You'll notice that all of the tried-and-true methods were free. While the most elaborate market research may still prove them the best, they can be refined continually, like your system. As you use your system to market your services, make marketing a part of your system.

Marketing to other financial advisors is a two-way street. You would not want to refer your clients to someone you did not know and trust. The same is true for the other advisors in making referrals to you. Take the initiative in cultivating relationships with the other advisors you meet in the normal course of business and professional activities.

Structuring Your Office for Maximum Productivity

The framework through which your system functions must be carefully structured to accommodate it efficiently. For most fee-only planners, this will be the most frustrating task they ever undertake. Most entrepreneurs are more creative than attentive to detail, and they are perplexed when forced to deal with practical matters. The only facts and figures they want to pore over are those pertinent to a client's financial plan. They don't realize, at least at the outset, that the figures pertaining to their own business are more important to their personal success. As a planner, you can survive if a client's plan goes awry. You don't want this to happen, and you do everything you can to make sure it doesn't; but, once established, you can afford some misdirection and still survive. What you can't afford is for your own plan to go awry.

Your system needs to function much as an assembly line does, except that you can't afford any Monday or Friday quality and productivity ratios. You are struggling to build a Rolls-Royce, and, although supposedly hand tooled, those cars aren't built alone. You need responsible technicians at every station attending to every detail. So you begin by determining your personal requirements and analyzing what contributions each individual will have to make.

Inside versus Outside Experts

Don't hire inside experts. Retain them, pay them a fee, reward them with referrals, or let them service you on speculation, but don't hire them. They will inhibit your growth, drain your resources, and breed discontent. If things start off well, they will want to become partners; if not so well, every other pasture will look greener. They will not be conducive to creation of the proper atmosphere within which the well-oiled machine must function. Remember from whence they come—of a fee-based and commission persuasion.

If circumstances make it necessary to have this expertise in-house, first determine whether the individual would like to leave what he or she is doing and start a fee-only practice in partnership with you: equal shares for equal investments. Then refer to Chapter 10 in this book, "Bringing in a Partner."

If your practice grows to the size where inside experts can be absorbed into the firm, make sure the expert is better than you in what he or she does. Then learn everything you can from the person, because that's what he or she will do with regard to your own expertise. It's not a level of expertise they will learn from you; it is how to handle the clients and the system that he or she will likely steal.

Instead of hiring in-house experts and running the risk of grooming your own competitors, utilize the expertise that placed itself at your disposal at the time of your transition—your specialists, the people who agreed to provide for you from their professions. If you are deserving of their time, they will be there for you because they will benefit, too. I've compensated my specialists—attorneys, brokers, agents, bankers, and accountants—and our relationships (and businesses) have flourished. We found it mutually beneficial to broker our services as professionals in our own fields and to concentrate on the portions of the planning process we have mastered. This won't usually be the case at the outset, but the quality fee-only planner can make it evolve. The important thing is that your specialists are in place when you begin.

You will need attorneys for review of documents and estate matters, and accountants for their expertise in taxes and shelters. I pay those people out of my fee, and I don't bill the client the expense. It's part of what I said I would provide in the absence of client advisors. You will need brokers to appraise product portfolios, but over time a deal can usually be worked out here as part of the broker's prospecting costs. Insurance professionals will be needed to review current policies and evaluate future needs, but their fees, too, are negotiable. An expert on employee benefits should carefully examine retirement, profit-sharing, medical, and disability plans for your corporate clients.

As part of your continuing education program, you will try to master some of these areas so you can provide more of these services yourself, while never losing sight of the fact that specialists are licensed professionals whose seal of approval is a necessity. Your system, functioning smoothly, is a very good marketing tool for these outside experts. Since these individuals helped grease the skids, don't neglect them, or others, in your future plans. Establish relationships with bankers and real estate professionals so that you can draw upon their expertise when needed. A true fee-only planner never unbundles his or her services, for any reason. You are coordinating the entire planning process, so you are responsible for attending to all contingencies. You've got to get the assembly line started, and the best way is to do it right the first time.

Setting Up Shop

Consistent throughout the development of your practice are two considerations: (1) structure for *quality*, and (2) structure for *efficiency*. Underlying these two is a third, a heartbeat behind in importance: structure for *harmony*. It all begins with you. What do you require? What can you afford? Start with a self-appraisal of your skills. What kind of assistance will you need? Supplemental, to improve your services? Complementary, to broaden them? What about support personnel? Is a secretary your first priority? An office manager? All of the above? You should have lists of things that need to be accomplished that can be transcribed into job categories for a manual. Prioritize your categories. What things can you do and still plan? What things can't you plan without? Where can you find the people to provide these services and reflect well on the image you strive to project? In general, I believe in paying people well. I think you should hire the best and compensate them accordingly. Often, you will save the cost of money and time to train a new employee or independent contractor.

The first person you hire could be the most important, so be very selective. A lot of fee-only people already have a person lined up to provide support when they make the transition. Too often, not enough research is put into this selection. The person is chosen simply because he or she is available or is a friend or relative. Then, six weeks into the practice the planner has to hire another person to support the first. That happened because *the planner* was unprepared, not the person who was hired, and the planner has made the first big mistake. You see how labor costs can mushroom. Carefully select someone who can perform all of the assigned tasks and more. Consider attitude, manner, appearance, and ambition. You must create the want in that person to direct him or her into sharing your goals. This someone can be a part-time student, depending on the responsibilities you assign. But in that case, you will have to accept the problem that students generally will be around for only a brief time. This turnover could be costly.

Base your hiring decision on what you need the most to put your business plan into action, and choose the person who can provide the most of what you need. Job descriptions can help you solidify your needs. With me, it was a secretary who not only had clerical skills, but also could handle scheduling, reception duties, and business matters. This mix of skills allowed her to evolve into my office manager; in fact, she set the tone for my whole business. She could perform functions I was weak in, thereby freeing me up to do what I do best.

The big advantage the first key person affords you is that between the two of you, you will have handled everything yourselves in the beginning and can teach the others exactly how you want things done. So make sure the first person you hire is right for you. Then build around that person.

A well-established fee-only planner's practice or partnership may consist of the following personnel:

- Planner or partner—to share ownership responsibilities

- Business manager—in charge of office business, such as client billing

- Director of operations—in charge of work flow

- Analyst supervisor—to provide cash flow analysis for clients

- Four to five analysts (possibly interns)—to analyze client data

- Data entry operator (depending on level of computerization)

- Receptionist

Everyone's duties need to be sharply defined in a manual, and people must be *shown*, not merely told, how they are expected to perform. You need to be an active employer and anticipate the changes and additions necessary for your staff. Each employee must understand how vital his or her function is to the overall process, because getting the job done will ultimately be as easy or as hard as each person along the assembly line wills it to be.

If you don't take time to do this, your employees will not be compatible. If you do, and if you give enough attention to trimming the rough edges, you will have laid the foundation for precision hand tooling and a harmonious environment. Getting off to a good start is important. People gain in confidence when they do something right the first time. This will be hard to do, but it also will never be easier to do because you will have fewer people and problems to deal with when you are starting out.

I'm very fortunate to have a great team that has been together for quite a while. They can run my system smoothly while accommodating the personnel changes common to any business. We have confidence in each other's abilities, and we take pride in our plans.

My key people have been in place long enough not only to master their duties, but also to cover for each other when necessary. This enables them to add a little more knowledge to their repertoire while gaining respect for another person's function. Since my system is well structured and functions smoothly because of its human components, our services have matured to the point that we can offer *more to more for more*, harmoniously.

As with most of my clients, most of my staff members were referrals from those already on board or from my specialists. I like that method because if a person likes to work with another, it's usually a pretty strong endorsement. Nobody wants a bad reference forever reflecting on his or her good judgment when that person sees the boss every day. However, getting the right people is so important that I wouldn't discount any manner of access. One advantage of an employment agency is that you're less likely to attract a client offspring or a friend of a friend, where your objectivity is possibly compromised. Whatever method you choose, remember that in selecting people to fill out your staff, *background is not as important as intelligence and character.*

Once you have assembled, assigned, and trained your staff, establish a regular line of communication to keep things in hand. At first, not only the process but also the people will be unfamiliar to everyone, and, when faced with the unfamiliar, people become tentative and hesitant—they keep things to themselves. A good environment will alleviate some of this, but the rest will have to be drawn out of the individuals. Thus, much attention must be given to staff meetings, which should be held at least once a week. Apply the same techniques you use with prospective clients—ask questions like "What documents will need to be verified on page X on the checklist?" Educate, don't admonish. Encourage questions in return. This should be a learning session for everyone. Make yourself available at a certain time each day for follow-ups or suggestions. Let everyone contribute. You will be too close to the field to see a lot of the action; you'll have to get things synchronized as quickly as possible.

Setting Goals for Your Business

An effective manager organizes and directs the available resources to achieve the goals of the organization. Those resources are human (professional and support), physical (furniture and equipment), and capital (yours, for the business, and the clients', for their plans). Management requires *planning*, to determine the goals of the organization and to set objectives that should be accomplished on the way to meeting those goals; *organization*, which includes the positioning of resources to enable the goals to be achieved; *implementation* of each of the activities designed to achieve the goals; and *control*, exercised on a day-to-day basis. The creation of an environment that allows the internal networking to evolve cohesively will determine the success of the fee-only firm.

As you establish yourself and begin to grow, adhere to your goals and objectives—don't randomly change them with whatever appears on the horizon. Your clients might continually adjust their goals for the first few years, and their plans will suffer; have enough sense to know that yours will, too. I can speak of this firsthand.

Starting out, flush with successful ventures, I became an empire builder, the country's largest. My original goal was to be successful, establish myself as a fee-only planner, and establish fee-only planning as a profession. As my then partners and I grew, we never formally redefined our goals and objectives. Our blueprint became obsolete, yet we kept on building and lost sight of our original goals. When we finally sat down to take stock and determine the cost of this oversight, vast discrepancies on our balance sheet became apparent, due *not* to our abilities as planners, but to our inattention to *our own* plans. The project had to be dismantled at great personal cost to me. The positive is that the system I created still functions successfully with the firm I founded and then left.

This is why, as you'll learn in Chapter 10, I'm not an indiscriminate advocate of partnership in practice. You can provide high-quality, personal, professional service on a consistent basis to enough people to be richly rewarded. When you have achieved your goals, take stock, and decide if you wish to establish new ones. No doubt you will, but don't modify them for your convenience in midstream.

Administrative and Professional Management

There are two facets to the management of a financial planning office: *administrative* and *professional*. The former involves those functions necessary to operate the planning firm as a business; the latter controls the planning process itself.

Administrative

Administrative management functions include personnel management, financial management and control, the supervision of operation of administrative systems, the purchasing of office supplies and equipment, and office space planning and administration. Attendant to these general categories of responsibility are the tasks required to establish any business; so, of the two facets, the business manager must have the more well-structured background because these are the areas in which the planner will be less likely to help, and the ones where the planner is more in need of assistance.

When starting your fee-only planning business, you will need to provide for yourself all the things you once took for granted. Remember, though, you don't need everything all at once. Too many beginning planners think they do and are immediately choked off by an income squeeze. Still, besides an office, office equipment, and supplies, you will need a telephone; licenses; insurance; parking facilities; and money for salaries, taxes, printing, postage, and other expenses.

If you want your practice to grow, you will have to find a business manager to take care of day-to-day office matters. There are a lot of competent business managers out there, but not many are available at the level of compensation you will be able to offer initially. You might need to find one who can complement your system and grow with the business. That person will learn by doing, will feel a part of your growth, and will be able to shape the skills and attitudes of your future employees—if you take the time to foster the proper working relationship in the beginning.

This person will have a lot to learn along with the opportunities you provide. He or she will eventually need to hire, train, discipline, and fire employees; evaluate their performance and maintain their records; develop budgets for income, expense, and capital items; control cash flow and disbursements; supervise bookkeeping; work with the firm's accountants to ensure timely preparation of financial statements and tax returns; take charge of billing, indexing, timekeeping, purchasing, and tenant-landlord relationships.

These functions are critical and become increasingly time-consuming as your practice grows. If your business manager cannot grow with them, your own growth will be retarded, and you will have to justify the additional expense to hire an experienced and qualified person.

Professional

Professional management functions entail the *distribution of work flow* to ensure that a firm brings its best resources to bear upon a client problem, the *monitoring of workloads* to ensure that they are evenly distributed, the *training and continuing education* of the staff, and the *control over the quality* of the work product.

This person will supplement your system. You will be able to perform all of these functions yourself, so you can teach at a faster pace. This director of operations, or professional manager, will probably be the second priority. Here, background is not as critical as it is for the administrative manager; but this person, too, will need to be a very capable administrator because he or she will be in charge of that precious commodity—time. Scheduling blocks of time for every task for every client with each planner and analyst not only allows the process to proceed according to schedule, but it is also the very essence of efficiency and professionalism. Done properly by experienced hands, the allocation of blocks of time for performance by the planners and their staff translates directly into profit for the firm.

Beyond management, certain staffing requirements will develop as you grow. Priorities should be set for each position according to its contribution to the quality and efficiency of your system. Most of the dead time in the planning process is due to the laborious chores of data gathering, organizing data, and developing a cash flow worksheet. Nearly all your clients will need assistance in one or all of these categories. It is your responsibility to see that they get it. I've found that each analyst can accommodate from 20 to 25 cases, so my professional manager hires on that rate. My analysts come from diverse backgrounds; about all they have in common is that they are conscientious, competent people, but this quality also can be found in an intern aspiring to fee-only planner status.

On your road to full computerization, a data entry operator will be essential, especially as you customize the software to your system. Clerical tasks will need several full-time attendants, which may be split up among either administrative assistants or secretaries. I like the administrative assistant method because these people will have both business and professional duties and will thus become knowledgeable about both facets of their place of employment, giving them a fuller understanding of the system.

In many ways, your receptionist is your best advertising investment. He or she makes a direct impression on each individual with whom you come in contact. From the people who call after seeing your listing in the phone book, to the prospective client from one of your seminars, to the most senior client on your roster, the receptionist sets the tone of your practice. He or she qualifies, exacts information, and introduces the rudiments of your service over the phone; assists clients in the office; and sets the standard for in-house public relations. If the receptionist personifies your professional image, there can be no significant gap in the social graces of the remainder of the staff. The whole staff must project an image that will maintain your clients' confidence in their selection of a financial planner.

Computerizing Your System

A great many changes have occurred in this area of financial planning in the past few years. They are not necessarily good. You cannot ignore the impact computers are having on our business, but I know very successful planners today who still do exemplary plans for their clients with a pen and calculator.

Remember you cannot make a quality computer decision until you know what you need from it. Therefore, at the time your financial planning system is in place, and *not before*, it will be necessary to buy a computer.

Software

There are many software packages available to the planner today. Some, such as Morningstar, have proven very valuable in serving clients. Others are smoke and mirrors or are cumbersome and aren't worth the money. They defeat the promise of a paperless society. It seems the attitude is: Overwhelm them with reports and graphs because they are there.

You will need basically to design your own software. The best software package currently available is Quicken for general financial organization, investment tracking, and reporting to the client. Reasonably priced, it allows the flexibility to modify according to your needs, as it was designed primarily for consumer use. Using this program could also prove beneficial as the client becomes more computer literate. Although we are currently using Quicken, we believe we have found a comprehensive financial planning software that will meet all our needs. Visit our Web site (www.sestina.com) for more information.

The day will come when the client will do all the grunt work on his or her computer and put the data on a floppy disk or Web site, and you will review the data for recommendations. Clients will mechanically analyze their own investments. Trading over the Web has only begun. The good news in this potential is that your staffing requirements should diminish. Also, you will be doing what you really want, which is dealing directly with the client and making meaningful recommendations to affect the client's life.

You will want antivirus protection software. Some will purchase specific asset allocation software. You will want a PIM (personal information manager) such as Outlook or Act to organize your calendar and addresses as well as other information. NAPFA planners are developing creative software solutions to aid you as well. There are financial planning spreadsheet templates and administrative software packages available for sale by these members.

Other systems supposedly designed for financial planners usually fall short in that they are too expensive and too product-oriented. They are more suited to sales and the offices of fee-based and commission-only planners. Batch processes are slow, restrictive, and inflexible. You need the computer to help you develop the plan according to your system. There's one basic plan, big client or small, so keep it simple. That's all you need and that's all the client wants. During your transition to computerization, continue to run your manual system concurrently with the computer system as a check until you are comfortable with the changeover.

Hardware

At this time, any IBM-compatible computer will suffice. As you purchase this equipment, realize the most important features are memory and speed. Depending on your practice, you will need a notebook computer or a desktop computer. Follow the most important rules about computers: first, plug it in; second, turn it on; and finally, back it up. Back it up as often as needed to ensure that if the worst happens and your system crashes, you minimize your downtime. Only you can determine if you should back up once a day or more often. Buy a piece of equipment for backing up. Today devices like Jazz drives provide significant disk space for quick backup. A color printer is essential. A multipurpose device that prints, scans, and faxes is inexpensive and gives you the best flexibility. Earlier I mentioned you should consider scanning documents. This keeps everything at your fingertips without searching through cumbersome binders or files. Organize your scanned information by client and in folders that correspond to your financial planning book you give the client. Identify each scanned document the same way you do in the financial software. For example, I use the symbols H, W, and J to identify husband, wife, and jointly owned. Therefore, I list a brokerage account as Schwab—H in the financial software and the same in the scanned folder. Consistency will save you time. Just like efficient time management, good organizational habits are invaluable.

Every year I back up everything on recordable CDs. This creates a permanent annual resource that takes up very little storage space.

Local Area Networks and the Internet

Some will decide to use local area networks (LANS). Be sure you hire competent individuals to install and set this up. You can use the Internet for free or subscription cost to create the same effect. Currently, Web sites like Visto.com and HotOffice.com provide some intranet capabilities. The advantage of using an intranet (a network between your associates) is the ability to share working files. However, you must set it up so that one person is responsible for the integrity of that file and the others use it in "read-only" mode or follow a specific format for attaching comments or changes to the file.

Naturally, you will need an Internet connection from an ISP (Internet service provider) and e-mail source. You will find more of your clients using e-mail as an effective communication tool.

I believe you *will* need to computerize your system, so plan accordingly. Refine your system and determine your needs. Make sure your computer doesn't dictate to you. Consider your future needs and each machine's adaptability to them. Use the three basic software programs—word processing, database management, and spreadsheet analysis—and your computer will be of great assistance in ensuring that your fee-only practice will be of high quality, efficient, and profitable.

Bringing In a Partner

I'm not overstating the case when I say that as much care should be taken in selecting a business partner as selecting a spouse. The two relationships have much in common. A bad partnership can impact a marriage as much as a bad marriage can impact a partnership. Many people get married or take on partners for the wrong reasons, or without knowing enough about themselves or their partner. In addition, some people just are not meant to have marital or business partners.

The differences between the two relationships reside primarily in the selection process. The choosing of a spouse is basically an emotional experience. Despite the fact that roughly half of today's marriages will end in divorce, few people give any thought to a prenuptial agreement or terms of separation. The selection of a business partner, however, should be the most selfish decision you ever make. Most fee-only planning entrepreneurs have economy-size egos, and in this instance they are usually better off to give in to their egos. Despite what I have said throughout about the value of interpersonal relationships, this is one time when you and your prospective business partner should be totally frank with each other. For a partnership to develop and prosper, all cards must be on the table, face up, jokers included, at the outset when the relationship is at its harmonious zenith.

The Psychological and Financial Aspects

Group practice seems more inevitable than ever before. Skyrocketing equipment costs, mounting operational expenses, and the proliferation of professionals are making the independent, single-practitioner office less viable. A recent study by Undiscovered Managers, a consulting group in Dallas, Texas (Mark P. Hurley et al., *The Future of the Financial Advisory Business and the Delivery of Advice to the Semi-Affluent Investor*, September 1999) suggests the small, one-person office will go the way of the dinosaur. More professionals are bringing in associates and partners to relieve the economic pressures and to share the time commitment necessary to maintain a practice. The psychological and financial ramifications of bringing in a new colleague are often overlooked when contemplating the benefits a new professional brings to the practice. They become areas of concern only when challenges arise.

As with any meaningful relationship, a partnership requires open, honest communication and progression through periods of development. Integrity, respect, and maturity are essential.

The Courtship

Before taking on a partner, think about fundamental questions such as: Why do you wish to be associated with this professional? (Answering this question requires an evaluation of the proposed partner and of you.) Where does this person fit in the relationship? When can he or she contribute? Will he or she supplement or complement the process? Will the person be cost-effective and/or result-effective? Will the person work well with the current staff and clients? Does he or she even aspire to be a partner?

You can evaluate the answers to these questions through introspection and observation. Both of you will need to determine your goals. The person might prefer to remain an employee without sharing responsibility for the business side of the practice, in which case offering a partnership relationship can do more harm than good. Adjustments need to be made with the addition of a new business associate. How willing is everyone to adapt? Will the changes result in better service to the clients? Weigh all the positive and negative effects, and try to analyze the proposed partner's willingness to share the benefits, expenses, and direction of the practice.

Test the relationship. Although the employer-employee environment is not an ideal format for testing a partnership relationship, it might be the only indicator available. Some planners prefer employees to partners. Employees always have their game face on to impress their employers, and they tend to be less improvisational. Give it time; let the answers come to you. Most professionals offer a share in the business too soon. A partnership offer should be made only after the associate has *asked* to be a partner. If the offer is made too soon, the new partner may experience the whole gamut of feelings from overwhelmed to indispensable, and the planner may later reflect that if the new partner didn't have the strength to ask for the relationship he or she doesn't add much strength to it. I personally feel that if any other way exists to accomplish your goals *without* offering a partnership, don't offer it.

The Proposal

Assuming the courtship of the prospective partner has endured for a reasonable amount of time, and both parties have decided that the relationship is mutually beneficial, it is time to formulate the proposal. Many partnership offers are both premature and excessively generous, perhaps because we are trained to care for others. In this aspect, we should care just as well for ourselves, making sure that the offer does not contain too much too soon. Justifying the merits of a possible association to trusted advisors and to your spouse will be beneficial because they can look at your decision critically and objectively. They may foresee the new relationship taking away from your income or adding to your administrative and financial burdens instead of affording you the benefits you imagined. Their input on this matter is much like the service you as a fee-only planner provide in the screening of investment opportunities for your clients. They can add objective insight because they are not directly representative of either side and are not as close to the situation.

Once you decide to proceed, determine a price. There are several textbook formulas for pricing a practice, but the reality is that it can be sold for whatever someone is willing to pay. Concrete factors in the valuation are the assets already owned and the receivables already created, but there is much more. Counsel with business and legal advisors should be closely interwoven in the evaluation process. Such matters are their professions, and they can also serve as mediators to counter any emotionalism that creeps in. As professionals, they, too, should be objective. Much as in setting fees, don't be afraid to ask a price that represents the total accumulated worth that portion of your practice has to you. It's up to the prospective partner to decide if it has that worth to him or her. *Then* you begin to negotiate. Evaluate first; negotiate second.

When a price is agreed upon, what is the method of payment? There are three possible choices: lump sum, installments, and salary reductions. Only the first is acceptable. Psychologically, for both parties, the best method is the lump-sum payment. There is more to buying something than merely agreeing to purchase. It's not yours until it's paid for. In my opinion, a prospective partner who doesn't have the money to make the lump-sum payment should either borrow it or buy a smaller portion of the business until he or she can afford to pay for more.

By-products of the remaining payment schedules can adversely affect the practice, and it's the little things that start wars. Just as monthly billings provide the client with 12 opportunities to wonder whether your services are worth it, monthly installments or monthly salary reductions give the new partner a chance to question the wisdom of his or her investment. Sooner or later, the partner concludes that the agreed-upon price is too much. Compounding the problem is the fact that you have to work *with* the partner, as opposed to *for* the client. In some area, performance suffers. The partner thinks he or she is working harder than you are, but taking home less.

How much of the practice should the new partner own? The prenuptial agreement says, "Let's be fair." In negotiation, when the word "fair" is uttered, everybody runs for cover. Is it fair for both partners to be equal when one has invested five or a dozen years building the practice? Do years of experience count? Sometimes professionals look for equal ownership because they think ownership designates salary. Salary has nothing to do with ownership. Contractually, income can be arranged that represents work effort without ownership consideration. Here again, competent, experienced advisors can provide impartial expertise and mediate the negotiations.

It is better for everyone to have separate advisors so that an advisor is not placed in a situation where he or she is more interested in compromise than in the client's best interests. Forging the partnership agreement will require hard-nosed negotiation and may indicate how the parties will react later. If the relationship cannot survive that initial round, it might not have survived for long anyway. An interesting way to test a relationship is with a "no." Disagreement can bring new insights. Test the relationship now, before it's too late.

When Challenges Begin: What Can Happen

In financial planning we have a saying, "The first year you bring in a partner, he loves you; the second year, he questions you; the third year, he resents you." The longer the new partner is around, the more incompetent you supposedly become, your comparative contributions are less, and the more unfairly he or she has been treated. Petty items grow into major obstacles. Writing a book, teaching a course, giving a lecture—are these endeavors contributing to or detracting from the firm? Does one person in the firm enjoy all the limelight while the partner labors in obscurity? Strained egos cause problems that can fester to the critical point. Attend to these problems at the source, before they become malignant. Remember this axiom: "Big egos make small problems big ones; small egos make big problems small ones"; and rare is the entrepreneur, or partner, with a small ego.

Then there are the expenses. What should the firm spend? Is a trip a qualified educational expense? Of course, unless the partner did not come. Does the revenue generated by one partner's lectures and seminars benefit the firm enough to warrant the expense? Is membership in a country club a legitimate expense if the partner does not golf? Who controls this? Is it work or play?

Responsibilities can become a way to assert control. The one who signs the checks is the boss and in control, at least in the eyes of employees and the recipients of the accounts payable.

Administration is another method of control. The large office and the bigger salary may not look quite so good if someone else can control a partner's time, work flow, and access to support personnel.

Still another form of control can be the relationship with these support personnel. Small cliques and loyalties can be developed. Other suspicions arise. Each partner begins to watch the time the other is working. Each counts the days of the other's vacation time or checks for liberties taken on expense accounts. It can go on and on.

Often the struggle becomes so great that it impedes the decision-making process. In this negative environment all decisions will require all partners, so all decisions can then die in committee. This puts each partner in the position of overriding the other when there is a disagreement. To overcome this problem, one of the partners may have to act as chief executive officer. In a group of super-egos this will be a difficult choice, and the negatives mount. It may be necessary to hire someone from outside, perhaps a member of your board, to serve in this capacity.

Clients can be an area of intense friction. Are they your clients, my clients, or the firm's clients? Who owns the files? This is a very sensitive area for not only partners, but clients as well. The clients' point of view must be the primary concern. The perception that they are being passed off to an underling must be avoided.

When you founded the firm, all the clients dealt with you; now you're asking them to counsel with somebody else. Why can't you continue as their advisor? Will this new person be as competent as you were? As caring? The prospect of interviewing with one partner and dealing with another puts some clients on guard. They are less willing to confide and more able to sense any undercurrent of dissent. The planning process suffers, and the seeds of dissatisfaction are sown. You will need to refine your system to prevent this from occurring.

What about outside investments? If financial opportunities are created for clients, does the firm or do the individual partners become eligible to join in the investment? What if one of the partners creates an unsuccessful investment venture?

Personal image can also cause concern. What if one partner likes to play donkey basketball? Is a philanderer? How is that image going to impair or impact the firm in the eyes of the other partner?

By this time, a "marriage counselor" may be in order. There are trained professionals who not only mediate partnership disputes but also facilitate communication and enhance the relationship. Look at what you've allowed to happen. The fee-only planner, the consummate communicator, the supreme coordinator, the person in charge is on the brink of collapse because of failure to do what he or she imperiously proclaims for others—plan.

The ultimate implementer is hamstrung in his or her own office, waiting for the shrink. The planner has lost control. It can happen. Perhaps you will find the outside counselor to be beneficial. Hopefully, all parties involved will feel the relationship is worth saving and will desire to work at it. Some partners, unfortunately, try to solve these problems by bringing in more partners to dilute them. It does not work.

Some Remedies; Few Cures

Interpersonal relationships are vital to the success of any partnership, but your relationship with a prospective partner has little to do with the one that develops with that same person as a partner. If the former relationship lacks the resiliency to withstand all that must be undergone to arrive at an equitable agreement, how can success be expected? If you can't work it out, don't enter in. When it is worked out, reexamine your goals and see if they are still compatible with the new arrangement. They probably won't be.

If the terms of the new partnership don't allow you to achieve the purpose of the partnership, don't agree to them. Even the best partnerships are short-term in this business because it is best suited to relatively small groups and large egos.

Here's one final point on human nature, reflecting back on the elements of the partner selection process. In any successful partnership, marriage or business, 50–50 or otherwise, someone is always in control, whether he or she knows it or not. In a business partnership, it is the person who is asked. Even if you need the prospective partner more than he or she needs you, find a way to create the want in him or her to ask for the partnership. That puts you in the driver's seat, initially at least.

Use the professionals from the outset. Just as 30 years ago there were no common denominators for credible market research, the value of what fee-only practices there were could not be accurately appraised. While all the measuring ability that's desirable is still not fully available, various standards have been set and formulas derived. Let both parties' respective attorneys and business specialists work up the parameters. It has been said that two un-knowledgeable people in discussion will argue, while two knowledgeable people will negotiate.

Be careful, however, that your professionals don't progress independently of your scrutiny and assign worth to the symbols in the formulas based on their experience in appraising, accounting, or medical practices. No tried-and-true method of measuring the worth of a roster of clients is available for financial planning practices, so this is the prime negotiable item in the proposal. My advice is that if two or more fee-only planners under the guidance of two teams of partnership counselors can't derive the value of the business they seek to divide, the relationship is best not entered into in the first place. Those business assets will only devaluate if left to be worked out after the partnership arrangement.

Predetermine everything, even the unforeseen. For example, methods of compensation: Are they equal or split according to production? Who owns the files? How will decisions be made? What if someone wants out? Dies? Becomes disabled? What if someone has to be put out? What about deferred compensation? What if you want part of your salary to accumulate as part of the business? And what if as a result of your accumulation, you create taxation in the business? Who pays that tax? How is it handled? Does that hamper the performance and flexibility of the other partner(s) involved? What about fringe benefits and pensions? What if you want to save more of your money?

What we've found to be successful is the piece-of-the-pie concept. If you can agree on what the overhead is, there is another piece left over that I'll call profit, recognizing it's not real profit. If there are two of you, split it in half. Then allocate those pieces accordingly. One can put 70% in the pension plan and keep 30% in salary. The other may want 90% in salary and 10% in insurance, with no pension. This is one flexible and effective alternative that should be predetermined. What about overhead? What constitutes profit?

The "marriage counselors" can have little effect when problems arise if all this has been neglected. The personalities involved will not be receptive; they are not the same people who made the agreement.

The most important part of any long-term relationship is knowing the other person. But before you rate the other person, probably the most important individual to understand is yourself. And as part of understanding yourself, you have to address what kind of business you wish to participate in. By that I mean, are you the kind of individual who wants to deal with a handful of clients on a close personal basis and has no interest in building a business empire? If that's true, don't bring in a partner.

If, on the other hand, you're the kind of person who dreams of an empire, you will need an expansion plan, and you will have to identify what kind of clientele you want to work with. Do you want to work with professionals? Corporations? Business executives? Do you want clients with strong egos, like yourself? Or do you need someone in the business with you who can buffer your ego and make it easier for clients to relate to the firm? You must determine the type of person you are and the type of business you have.

You also must consider your strengths and weaknesses. Personally, I'm very excited about meeting new clients, marketing financial planning, and solving people's problems. However, I've never been interested in the nitty-gritty detail—that's the function of my analysts and support personnel. So my system allows me to operate much like a neurosurgeon who performs surgery after all the preparatory stages have been attended to. The people around me supplement my skills. They are better than me at what they do, which allows me to concentrate on what I do best. I trained them by showing them what I require to operate after having determined my strengths and weaknesses by doing everything myself in the early days. All the details and preparations are given expert attention, but not by me. Today you can do everything yourself, but remember one thing in financial planning—earn a living.

Conversely, the empire builders will want people to complement their skills so the firm can see more people and do more cases. They will need supplementary personnel, too, just as I need people to complement me, but they are more vulnerable to partnership problems. I was an empire builder in my first life, and I learned from my mistakes.

Whichever system you favor, evaluate the contributions of the people who enable it to function. Are those contributions significant enough for partnership consideration? Most financial planners know less about themselves and their practices than they know about others. Most of us don't have our own goals and our own financial plans, so choosing a business partner is a difficult process. You have to devise ways to measure competency and complementary and supplementary attitudes. You must be sure of your objective in bringing in this person. I had two objectives in my current partnership venture. I was tired of working 60 to 80 hours a week, yet I wanted to maintain my level of income. If I could accomplish this and maintain my quality of service by bringing in partners, it was worth it to me.

However, will this person generate more income or detract from your current income? Can you afford it financially? Psychologically? Maybe you want to bring in a partner to share overhead and cut expenses. It gets very expensive to have a sophisticated system in operation. Mine would cost about $2 million to start today. As you're growing, you may want to bring someone in to man the presses, so to speak, and crank out income while you're building the practice. In such a case, a partnership may be your only refuge, but it is no less an important decision.

So treat yourself as you treat your clients. Sort yourself out. Establish your goals and the methods of progression. Partnership in practice is a monumental decision regarding a proposed relationship that should be considered with all the seriousness it deserves. Use the questions posed in this chapter to evaluate more than just the financial aspects of your proposed or present relationship. Use your own professional insight to help you determine the relative worth of partnership in practice.

Many alternatives to group practice have arisen. Outright acquisition by another firm is one possibility. It is tempting to be offered a large amount for your practice as well as stock in the acquiring company. In addition to the issues already raised for a partnership, consider these questions: Do you need to feel independent in your business? How do you feel about working in a corporate environment? Can you deal with bureaucratic thinking? What if you are told to change long-term beliefs about how a client should be handled? Are you willing to respond to the concerns of the shareholders?

My approach to the need for a larger organization has been to create a network of independently owned financial planning offices (Sestina Network of Fee-Only Financial Planners). Planners from all backgrounds have joined to learn the process of successful fee-only financial planning. This association gives them the advantage of a large organization without the limitations of a corporate environment.

First I require they train with me and other planners in the network to learn the fundamentals regarding the process. They attend client meetings to observe how to deal with the prospect and then the client. They participate in the implementing of the client's needs. This experience allows them to ask questions while they learn. They are expected to get their own clients, but I am able to refer them a few clients in the beginning. Should they get off to a slow start I am willing to pay them to assist me with my clients. The goal, however, is for them to be on their own. They can network with the other planners and share one another's areas of expertise. We are also creating a back-office capability to do the less productive work. The planner is most profitable when dealing with the client, not ordering a form from a broker.

My experience has been interesting. As I said early on, my goal remains to create a profession. My effort with the network is to meet that objective. To that end, I teach these people my system. As of this writing I have 52 people I am seriously considering and a file cabinet drawerful of names I have rejected. As expected, I have had mixed results. Of those who have attempted it, the ones who did not have the entrepreneurial bent didn't make it. I've been given amazing reasons for discontinuing their offices. One individual told me he could not be alone. One said that, upon demand from him, he should be given clients he had trained on with me. Interesting, isn't it? People will always be people. While they are learning, they are excited about what they're doing; but as time passes . . . how did that go? . . . the first year they love you; the second year they question you; the third year they resent you.

Your choice of business is up to you. The profession needs many more committed, competent, comprehensive fee-only financial planners. I wish you well.

Fees

How do I charge for my services?

This question continues to frustrate many new and experienced planners. Back in the dark ages when I started in 1965 no one knew what a financial planner was, let alone a fee-only planner. As a result, over the years, I have had to experiment with about every conceivable manner of charging there is.

In the beginning I charged commissions only. It was logical for the time. Gradually, I attempted charging a small fee for writing the plan. The commissions earned through the recommendations paid for the cost of implementation.

From there as I evolved closer to a fee-only arrangement, I charged a total fee that could be offset by any commissions generated. For example, if my fee was $10,000 and commissions were $2,000, then the client would pay $8,000. This was not satisfactory, as the commissions could always be structured to exceed the calculated fee.

When I made the determination to be fee-only, I first went to the hourly charge. I soon realized I could never be fully compensated for my efforts with this method. First of all, I could never bill for all the work done on behalf of the client. Researching investments for clients could not be divided up fairly among them, for example. Second, I learned the clients did not like hourly charges. They never knew what the total cost was going to be. Just as we experience when we receive bills from hourly professionals, there was some skepticism regarding a bill that represented research or some other esoteric work. Laughingly they might ask whether I needed a new set of tires for my car with such a bill. The other risk to me was that there was no income when a client had to cancel a meeting.

Next, I tried to bill a flat fee for each part of the service. There was a charge for writing the plan, another for implementation, and another for annual review. Once again, the clients would now make choices about the services they required based on cost. In addition, it caused them to improperly evaluate whether they needed the next step. We know they need the whole process: plan, implement, and review.

Next, I tried billing based on the number of client meetings held per year. They could choose among monthly, quarterly, or semiannual meetings and would pay accordingly. Once again, this was not beneficial to the clients or to me because it allowed them to make the choice. The choice was generally based on their perception of need, not on what they really needed.

At a meeting with Bob Underwood, he explained a billing system that seemed to make sense. Bill on the only measurable tangibles the client and you could identify—earned income and investments. I explain to a prospective client that this is an unscientific attempt to measure the work involved. And it is. When I determine that the fee is excessive for the anticipated work, I adjust it downward by reducing percentages or eliminating the earned income portion of the fee. I explain to them the first several years will be the most work-intensive for me. There seems to be a correlation between the level of earned income and time required. More time is required of the planner as opposed to staff with higher-income individuals. During this time there are more organizational requirements.

By the same token, I wish to be compensated for my success in each case and penalized for lack of success. I do not want to be distracted by continually looking for new clients, and I want to grow with my clients; I want a long-term relationship. I use a different schedule for self-employed individuals as opposed to employees, as there is more time required for a self-employed individual. Finally, they know what the total cost will be. There are no extras—no faxing or telephone charges. In addition, I am not put in the position of renegotiating a fee every year with the client. The client knows the formula in advance and can anticipate the cost. Naturally, there is a minimum charge. This minimum prevents your fee from going to an unacceptable level after a few years.

From my point of view, this approach eliminates wasted time detailing where my time is spent. This system has worked successfully since 1974.

The client is expected to pay 50% upon engagement, 25% in 90 days, and the balance 90 days later. This applies to new and renewed clients. Remember, each time the client receives an invoice from you he or she evaluates your service. Therefore, the fewer times you can send one, the better off you are.

One caution! This is not a fee on assets or investments managed. The percentage charged on investments includes all the client's investments, irrespective of who manages them. It is necessary to include them because you will be considering and monitoring all of those investments in the plan. Further, if this were a fee on only assets managed, it would be a conflict of interest. The conflict is your income. If you can convince the client to give you more assets to manage, your income increases. In so doing, you may be taking money from a better money manager than you.

The simple fee system worksheet is in Appendix B. You can use whatever percentages you feel comfortable using.

Some have taken this system and used the client's net worth instead of investments. They argue this prevents a conflict of not using money from investments for other personal needs (i.e., to reduce the mortgage. In my philosophy an investment is to be used only for future goals such as retirement or education. I insist the client use savings or other reserves for such things as vacations, new cars, mortgage reduction, and so on. In general, it is more beneficial financially to maintain a mortgage and invest rather than to reduce the mortgage. On rare occasions, it is beneficial to reduce the mortgage because the rate is extremely high. However, a well-educated client will recognize how to evaluate the after-tax cost/return of any investment or loan. All calculations should be done on an after-tax basis. Then the comparison is easy and logical.

Others have created more elaborate fee systems. Most have come to the conclusion an annual charge is best. They evaluate the staff requirements and estimate the time required of each of them. They calculate the fee per staff member. They may estimate the number of meetings they expect per year. It seems there is an administrative dollar and time cost in this approach or a variation of it.

Irrespective of the fee system you engage, make it clear in the appropriate materials that you can negotiate a different fee than the one you have published. Do not be too rigid in your fee system of choice. You will discover flexibility will prevent uncomfortable situations.

APPENDIX A

Confidential Questionnaire

DOCUMENTATION CHECKLIST

Check all which apply. Copies are acceptable, but if you provide originals, they will be returned to you at your next meeting.

Date   Pending   N/A
Received

TAX & INCOME INFORMATION

1 Federal Income Tax returns (Form 1040) and W-2's for the three (3) most recent years, including all children's tax returns.
2 State and Local Income Tax returns for the most recent year.
3 Two (2) most recent paycheck stubs.
4 IRS Form 2119 if you have sold a prior residence (attached to your federal tax return for the year in which you sold your residence)
5 Trust federal income tax return (Forms 1041 and K-1) from which you receive income or principal.

STATEMENTS—CASH, STOCKS, BONDS, ETC.

1 Most recent bank statement(s).
2 Savings statement(s)/passbook(s).
3 Certificate(s) of Deposit, or receipt(s) for purchase of CD(s).
4 Original purchase confirmations for stocks and bonds.
5 All statements for mutual funds since inception.
6 All brokerage statements for current year.
7 Confirmations for sale of any investments this calendar year.

OTHER

1 Deed(s) for all real estate owned, including residence.
2 Closing statement(s) for all real estate owned, including residence.
3 Mortgage note(s) for all real estate owned, including residence.
4 Most recent year-end statement of interest and principal paid on mortgage loan(s).
5 Most recent appraisal on all real estate owned.
6 Note(s) for loans owed by you and current balance(s).
7 Lease agreement(s) for all rental properties.
8 Prospectuses/Offering Memoranda for all investments (limited partnerships, etc.).

FIGURE A.1 Documentation Checklist

9 Subscription Agreements for all investments (limited partnerships, etc.).
10 Most recent K-1 form and financial statements for all partnerships owned.
11 Note(s) for loans owed to you.
12 All annuity contracts and most recent statement(s).
13 Information on investment options for variable annuities.
14 Record of past performance for variable annuity options.
15 Receipt(s) for purchase of gold/silver coins.

BUSINESS DOCUMENTS

1 Business federal tax returns for last three (3) years.
2 Most current business financial statements(s).
3 Employment Agreement(s).
4 Buy-Sell Agreement(s).
5 Partnership Agreement(s).
6 All agreement(s) for business property.
7 Deferred Compensation Agreement(s).

PLEASE PROVIDE THE FOLLOWING DOCUMENTS: INSURANCE

1 Insurance policies for the following:
   Homeowner's or Renter's
   Automobile
   Marine or Aircraft
   Umbrella
   Rental Property
   Office
   Professional Liability
   Retirement Plan Trustee Fidelity Bond
   Employee Bond(s)
   Life
   Disability
   Business Overhead
   Hospitalization
   Major Medical
   Dental
   Workers' Compensation certificate
   Other
2 Most recent premium notice, loan notices, dividend notice, and annual report, if applicable, for policies checked.

FIGURE A.1 *Continued*

3 All correspondence (as received) concerning insurance policies.
4 Summary Description of cafeteria plan & flexible spending account.

ESTATE DOCUMENTS
1 Wills.
2 Trust Agreement(s).
3 Power(s) of Attorney or Appointment.
4 Living will(s) and/or Durable Power(s) of Attorney for Health Care.
5 Letter of Instructions.

RETIREMENT PLAN DOCUMENTS
1 Summary Plan Description(s) for retirement plan(s).
2 Retirement Plan Participant Statement(s) or Allocation Statement(s) for the last plan year end and most recent investment return calculations.
3 Copies of beneficiary designations for all retirement plans.
4 Information on investment options for 401(k), 403(b), and Deferred Compensation plans.
5 Record of past performance for investment options of 401(k), 403(b), and Deferred Compensation plans.
6 Section 242(b) Election (to defer mandatory pay-out past age $70^1/_2$).
7 Grandfather Election (Form 5329 filed with 1988 tax return) for excess accumulations in retirement plans.

PERSONAL INFORMATION
1 Prenuptial Agreement(s).
2 Divorce/Dissolution Agreement(s).
3 Automobiles.
4 Automobile lease agreement(s).

Year	Make	Model	Owed on Value	Owed on Lease	Loan

FIGURE A.1 *Continued*

Personal Information

Legal Name	Birthdate	Social Security Number			
John Smith	12/12/12	111-22-3333			
Mary Smith	3/28/43				

Maiden Name	Jones

ADDRESS	Street	City	State	Zip	Phone
Residence	7677 Tamarisk Court	Dublin	OH	43016	(614) 798-1742
				FAX	
				FAX	
				E-mail	
				E-mail	

John Smith		Mary Smith	
Occupation		Occupation	
Employer		Employer	
Address		Address	
Phone		Phone	
FAX		FAX	
Title/Professional		Title/Professional	
Specialty		Specialty	
Date of Employment		Date of Employment	

CHILDREN

Name	Birthdate	Sex	Social Security Number	Marital Status	No of Children	Custody?
Example	12/12/12	M	123-45-6789	S	0	Y

PARENTS AND/OR DEPENDENTS

Name	Birthdate	Relationship		

ADDRESS	Street	City	State	Zip	Phone

Name	Birthdate	Relationship		

ADDRESS	Street	City	State	Zip	Phone

FIGURE A.2 Personal Information

Personal Advisors

Client: John Smith   Date: 9/7/00
          Mary Smith

Financial Planner

Name	Street	City	State	Zip	Phone	
John E. Sestina	7677 Tamarisk Court	Dublin	OH	43016	Office	(614) 798-1742
					FAX	(614) 792-5152
					E-mail	jsestina@sestina.com

Attorney

Name	Street	City	State	Zip	Phone	
					Office	
					FAX	
					E-mail	

Accountant

Name	Street	City	State	Zip	Phone	
					Office	
					FAX	
					E-mail	

Banker

Name	Street	City	State	Zip	Phone	
					Office	
					FAX	
					E-mail	

Stockbroker

Name	Street	City	State	Zip	Phone	
					Office	
					FAX	
					E-mail	

Trust Officer

Name	Street	City	State	Zip	Phone	
					Office	
					FAX	
					E-mail	

Life Insurance Agent

Name	Street	City	State	Zip	Phone	
					Office	
					FAX	
					E-mail	

Homeowners Insurance Agent

Name	Street	City	State	Zip	Phone	
					Office	
					FAX	
					E-mail	

FIGURE A.3 Advisor Summary

Personal Advisors

Client:	John Smith		Date:	9/7/00
	Mary Smith			

Automobile Insurance Agent

Name	Street	City	State	Zip		Phone
					Office	
					FAX	
				E-mail		

Medical Insurance Agent

Name	Street	City	State	Zip		Phone
					Office	
					FAX	
				E-mail		

Disability Insurance Agent

Name	Street	City	State	Zip		Phone
					Office	
					FAX	
				E-mail		

Clergy

Name	Street	City	State	Zip		Phone
					Office	
					FAX	
				E-mail		

Physician

Name	Street	City	State	Zip		Phone
					Office	
					FAX	
				E-mail		

Other

Name	Street	City	State	Zip		Phone
					Office	
					FAX	
				E-mail		

FIGURE A.3 *Continued*

Safe-Deposit Box and Marriage

Client	John Smith		Date:	9/7/00
	Mary Smith			

SAFE-DEPOSIT BOX INFORMATION

Name of Bank:

Bank Address: Street

City   State   Zip

Box in Name of:

Box Number:

Location of Box Keys:

CURRENT MARRIAGE

Date   City   State

PREVIOUS MARRIAGES

Dissolution Agreement

Date   City   State

Property settlements and/or premarital agreements

POTENTIAL INHERITANCE

Name   Amount

FIGURE A.4 Safe-Deposit Box and Marriage

Personal Goals Summary				
Area	*2000 Goals* 1 Year Commitments	Short-term Goals 2-4 Years	Mid-term Goals 5-10 Years	Life-time Goals > 10 Years
Personal	Need to work on	Need to work on	Need to work on	Need to work on
Professional 　　John	Start up business	Get back to old salary	Double old salary	Partially retire
Mary			Partially retire	
Financial				
Debts			Retire exp. debt	Retire home mortgage
Emergency Funds	Add $10,000	Add $10,000/yr	Maintain 50K equivalent	
Living Quarters	Good	Good	Good	Bigger/better house?
Vehicles	Good	Good	New BMW 740/50 ($65 equiv.)	Sports car $40k
Possessions	Good	Vacation home/ additional time share		
Vacations, Recreations, and Entertainment	2 wks	2 weeks/yr	3 weeks/yr	2 months/yr
Trip List 　(Where and When)	Indiana, Thanksgiving	Back to Europe	Back to Europe	World Travel
Retirement				Retire by 43 (H) Retire by 40 (W) Does QFP allow for partial retirement? (partially, both)
Gifts and Charities	Improve	Improve	Improve	Improve
Family 　(Other than above) 　Son				College/marriage
Other				

FIGURE A.5 Personal Goals Summary

Cash Flow Forecast

	Date		January	February	March	April	May	June	July	August	Sept	October	November	December	Current Lifestyle Total
Client	Birthdate														
John Smith	Birthdate														
Mary Smith		9/7/00													
1997 Cash Flow Forecast															
INCOME															
John Smith															
Mary Smith															
Rental Income															
Other															
Other															
TOTAL INCOME															
EXPENSES															
Accountant Fees															
Alimony Payments															
Attorney Fees															
Auto-Gas, Repairs, etc.															
Cable TV															
Charitable Contributions															
Child Support Payments															
Children's Day Care															
Children's Education - current															
Children's Education - future															
Clothing															
Country Club, Health Club, etc.															
Entertainment															
Financial Planner Fees															
Gifts/Celebrations															
Groceries															
Hobbies															
Home Furnishings															
Home Repairs/Maintenance															
Home Lawn Care															
House Cleaning															
Insurance Premium - Auto															
Insurance Premium - Boat/other															
Insurance Premium - Disability															
Insurance Premium - Home															
Insurance Premium - Life															
Insurance Premium - Umbrella															
Licenses															
Loan - Auto 1															
Loan - Auto 2															
Loan - Home Equity Payments															
Loan - Home Mortgage Payments															
Loan - Other															
Medical Insurance Premiums															
Medical/Dental Expenses															
Personal Allowances															
Rent															
Subscriptions															
Taxes - Income															
Taxes - Real Estate - Home															
Taxes - Real Estate - Other															
Utilities - Cable															
Utilities - Electric															
Utilities - Gas															
Utilities - Telephone															
Utilities - Water & Sewer															
Vacations															
Other															
IRA Contributions															
TOTAL EXPENSES															
SURPLUS															
CUMULATIVE SURPLUS															

FIGURE A.6 Cash Flow Forecast

110

FIGURE A.6 *Continued*

	Husband Passes Away	Husband Disabled	Spouse Passes Away	Spouse Disabled	Current Lifestyle	Retirement Lifestyle
Client						
John Smith						
Mary Smith						
1996 Cash Flow Projection						
INCOME	Total Life Insurance> H	Total Disability Inc - H	Total Life Insurance> W	Total Disability Inc - W	Total	Total
John Smith						
Mary Smith						
Rental Income						
Other						
Other						
TOTAL INCOME						
EXPENSES						
Accountant Fees						
Alimony Payments						
Attorney Fees						
Auto-Gas, Repairs, etc.						
Cable TV						
Charitable Contributions						
Child Support Payments						
Children's Day Care						
Children's Education - current						
Children's Education - future						
Clothing						
Country Club, Health Club, etc.						
Entertainment						
Financial Planner Fees						
Gifts/Celebrations						
Groceries						
Hobbies						
Home Furnishings						
Home Repair/Maintenance						
Home Lawn Care						
House Cleaning						
Insurance Premium - Auto						
Insurance Premium - Boat/other						
Insurance Premium - Disability						
Insurance Premium - Home						
Insurance Premium - Life						
Insurance Premium - Umbrella						
Licenses						
Loan - Auto 1						
Loan - Auto 2						
Loan - Home Equity Payments						
Loan - Home Mortgage Payments						
Loan - Other						
Medical Insurance Premiums						
Medical/Dental Expenses						
Personal Allowances						
Rent						
Subscriptions						
Taxes - Income						
Taxes - Real Estate - Home						
Taxes - Real Estate - Other						
Utilities - Cable						
Utilities - Electric						
Utilities - Gas						
Utilities - Telephone						
Utilities - Water & Sewer						
Vacations						
Other						
IRA Contributions						
TOTAL EXPENSES						
SURPLUS						
CUMULATIVE SURPLUS						

111

Asset/Lifestyle Accounts

| Client | John Smith | | | Date: | 9/7/00 |
| | Mary Smith | | | | |

Checking

Name on Account	Name of Institution	Account Number	Average Balance	Contact Person	Phone

Saving

Name on Account	Name of Institution	Account Number	Average Balance	Contact Person	Phone

Certificates of Deposit

Name on Account	Name of Institution	Account Number	Current Value	Maturation Date	Interest Rate

Fixed Assets

Asset	Owner	Estimated Value
Jewelry		
Furs		
Art Objects, collections		
Furniture		
Personal Property		

FIGURE A.7 Asset/Lifestyle Accounts

Vehicles					
Description Auto, boat, etc.	Vehicle Identification Number	Registered Owner	Title Location	Purchase Date	Fair Market Value

Intellectual Property				
	Owner	Annual Income	Expiration	Current Value
Patents				
Trademarks				
Copyrights				

Beneficiary or Remainder Interests in Trusts or Other Contract Rights

Give details of prospective profits, liabilities, and values involved

FIGURE A.7 *Continued*

Real Estate Interests

Client	John Smith Mary Smith			9/7/00

		1	2	3
1	Property Number			
2	Description	Residence		
3	Address Street City, State Zip			
4	Owner(s) and % Ownership			
5	Current Market Value			
6	Acquired From			
7	How Acquired (purchased, (gift, inheritance, etc.)			
8	Date Acquired			
9	Original Cost			
10	Cash Down Payment			
11	Amount Borrowed			
12	Cost of Improvements			
13	Second Mortgage Amount Borrowed			

14 Rental Properties: If any of the above are rental properties, please supply.

Tenant Name	
Date Leased	
Terms of Lease, Sq. Ft. Leased	
Monthly Rental	
Operating Expense	
15 Depreciation	
Basis	
Method	
Life	

FIGURE A.8 Real Estate Interests

114

Liabilities			
Client John Smith Mary Smith			9/7/00
Consumer Debt - Car Loans			

Car
Borrower
Date of Loan
Creditor
  Address
  City, State Zip
  Phone
Account Number
Original Amount
Payment
Payable
Payment Date
Interest Rate			

Equity Debt - Mortgages and Land Contracts			

Loan
Borrower
Date of Loan
Creditor
  Address
  City, State Zip
  Phone
Account Number
Original Amount
Payment
Payable
Payment Date
Interest Rate			

Equity Debt - Home Equity Loans/Second Mortgages			

Loan
Borrower
Date of Loan
Creditor
  Address
  City, State Zip
  Phone
Account Number
Original Amount
Payment
Payable
Payment Date
Interest Rate			

FIGURE A.9 Liabilities

Leases			
Item(s) Leased			
Lessee			
Date of Lease			
Lessor			
Address			
City, State Zip			
Phone			
Lease Number			
FMV of Items Leased			
Terms of Lease			
Lease Payment			
Taxes			
License Fees			
Security Deposit			
Renewal Option			
Buy-out Option			
Annual Mileage Limit			
Maintenance			
Insurance			
Payment			

FIGURE A.9 *Continued*

Credit Cards Summary

Client	John Smith	Date:	9/7/00
	Mary Smith		

Card Name	
Card Holder	
Date of Loan	
Creditor	
Address	
City, State Zip	
Phone	
Card Number	
Payment	
Payment Date	
Interest Rate	
Card Name	
Card Holder	
Date of Loan	
Creditor	
Address	
City, State Zip	
Phone	
Card Number	
Payment	
Payment Date	
Interest Rate	
Card Name	
Card Holder	
Date of Loan	
Creditor	
Address	
City, State Zip	
Phone	
Card Number	
Payment	
Payment Date	
Interest Rate	
Card Name	
Card Holder	
Date of Loan	
Creditor	
Address	
City, State Zip	
Phone	
Card Number	
Payment	
Payment Date	
Interest Rate	

FIGURE A.10 Credit Cards Summary

Investment Accounts

Client	John Smith Mary Smith					Date:	9/7/00

Tax Deferred

IRA

Name on Account	Current Value	Name of Institution	Account Number	Type of IRA	Beneficiary	Phone

Contribution History

For Year	Amount	For Year	Amount	For Year	Amount

Pension

Name on Account	Current Value	Name of Institution	Account Number	Beneficiary	Phone	Contact Person

Profit Sharing

Name on Account	Current Value	Name of Institution	Account Number	Beneficiary	Phone	Contact Person

Taxable

Brokerage Accounts, Mutual Funds, Stocks, Bonds, etc.

Name on Account	Current Value	Name of Institution	Account Number	Phone	Contact Person

FIGURE A.11 Investment Accounts

401(k) Summary		
Employee: Account Number: Company: Contact Person: Phone: Investment Advisor: Phone: Current Allocation: As Of: Other Inv. Options: Investment Changes: Current Contribution: Company Match: Loans Available: Beneficiary: As of: Contribution History		
Contribution History	Date Amount	Date Amount

FIGURE A.12 401(k) Summary

Business Interests Summary

(Enclose copies of tax returns, financial statements, employment agreement, buy-sell agreement, incorporation documents or partnership agreement, pertinent lease agreements.)

	1	2	3	4
Business Name				
Address				
Description of Business				
Federal ID No.				
Effective Date				
Fiscal Year End				

Business Type:				
Sole Proprietorship				
General Partnership				
Limited Partnership				
Regular Corporation				
Subchapter S Corporation				
Limited Liability Company				

Accounting Method:				
Cash Basis				
Accrual Basis				
Hybrid Basis				

Amount Invested $				
Amount Loaned $				

Shareholders or Partners Name(s)	No of shares/ Units	No of shares/ Units	No of shares/ Units	No of shares/ Units

Total Shares/Units Outstanding				
Number Shares/Units Authorized				

FIGURE A.13 Business Interests Summary

Directors

1				
2				
3				
4				
5				

Officers
President
Vice President
Secretary
Treasurer

Yes/No	Yes/No	Yes/No	Yes/No

Do you have an
employment agreement?

Do you have a buy-sell
agreement?

Have you established any
goals for your business?
If so, please discuss.

Fringe Benefits:
Automobile
Company loans
Stock options
Other

What is your estimate of
a fair market value for
your business?

How did you arrive at
this figure?

FIGURE A.13 *Continued*

Partnership Interest Summary

(Enclose copies of tax returns, financial statements, employment agreement, buy-sell agreement, incorporation documents or partnership agreement, pertinent lease agreements.)

	1	2	3	4	5	6
Business Name						
Owner						
Ownership %						
Units						
General Partner						
Description						
Federal ID #						
Effective Date						
Fiscal Year End						
Business Type						
Accounting Method						
Investment						
Date						
Amount						

FIGURE A.14 Partnership Interest Summary

Employee Census Information
For the 12-Month Fiscal Period

Employer:

IMPORTANT:

1. Include ALL employees who were employed at any time during the year.
2. Indicate in last column by an X anyone currently employed who was rehired after a period of employment.
3. "Hours of Service" means each hour for which an employee is directly or indirectly paid or entitled to payment for the performance of duties during the Plan Year.

| Employee | Sex | Office or Shareholder | Birthdate | Date of Hire | Social Security Number | Hours of Service | | | Compensation (income reportable for federal tax purposes for services during the compensation period) | | | | | Termination of Employment Mo/Day/Yr |
						500 or less	501 to 999	1,000 or More	Basic	Bonus	Overtime	Commission	Total	

FIGURE A.15 Employee Census Information

Property & Casualty Insurance

(Enclose actual individual and business insurance policies; most recent premium notice.)

	Yes	No	Documents Enclosed
Homeowners			
Renters			
Auto			
Office			
Business Interruption			
Employee Bonds			
Umbrella			
Professional Liability			
If Corporation, Corporation Professional Liability			
Retirement Plan Trustee Fiduciary Insurance			
Retirement Plan Trustee Fidelity Insurance			
Marine			
Aircraft			
Other			

FIGURE A.16 Property and Casualty Insurance

Life Insurance

(Enclose actual insurance policies or descriptive brochures and, if group, individual certificates; most recent premium notices. List policies on your life, your spouses, your children's, and your business associates' lives. If necessary, use back of this page.)

Insured	Insurance Company	Policy Number	Face Value	Policy Type	Documents Enclosed

FIGURE A.17 Life Insurance

Health Insurance

(Enclose actual insurance policies, descriptive brochures, individual certificates of insurance, most recent premium notices.)

	Man		Woman		Documents
	Yes	No	Yes	No	Enclosed

Hospitalization Insurance
Company
Premium Payor

Major Medical Insurance
Company
Premium Payor

Health Insurance on Employees,
if different from above
Premium Payor

Blue Cross/Blue Shield Numbers

Certificate Number
Group Number
Premium Payor

Medical Expense Reimbursement Plan
Insured?
Non-insured?

Dental - Vision Insurance
Company
Premium Payor

Long-Term Care Insurance
Company
Premium Payor

Other

FIGURE A.18 Health Insurance

Disability and Business Overhead Expense Insurance

(Enclose actual insurance policies, descriptive brochures, individual certificates of insurance, most recent premium notices.)

Insured	Insurance Company	Policy Number	Monthly Benefit	Premium Payor	Documents Enclosed

FIGURE A.19 Disability Insurance

Husband's Will

Testator	
Date Signed	
Executor	
Address	
City, State Zip	
Contingent Executor	
Address	
City, State Zip	
Guardian	
Address	
City, State Zip	
Asset Distribution Provisions	
Specific Assets	
Remainder	
Drafting Attorney	
Address	
Phone	
FAX	
E-mail	
Location of Document	

FIGURE A.20 Will—Husband

Wife's Will

Testator	
Date Signed	
Executor	
Address	
City, State Zip	
Contingent Executor	
Address	
City, State Zip	
Guardian	
Address	
City, State Zip	
Asset Distribution Provisions	
Specific Assets	
Remainder	
Drafting Attorney	
Address	
Phone	
FAX	
E-mail	
Location of Document	

FIGURE A.21 Will—Wife

Estate Planning

REVOCABLE TRUST

GRANTOR:

TRUSTEE(S):

SUCCESSOR TRUSTEE(S):

DATE:

INITIAL FUNDING:

Cash Deposit:	$ -	
Life Insurance:	Yes	No

UPON THE GRANTOR'S DEATH:

Trust assets to be divided into two (2) parts:
Trust A (1, Marital or spouse's) and
Trust B (2, Nonmarital, Residual, or Family)

ART. & PAR.

Credit Shelter Formula _____

TRUST A

All income to spouse _____

Spouse's right to withdraw all
Trust A assets _____

Spouse's limited right to withdraw
Trust A assets _____

Trustee's right to distribute all
Trust A assets _____

General Power of Appointment _____

FIGURE A.22 Revocable Trust

NAME:

TRUST B		ART. & PAR.
	All income to spouse	_____
	All income to spouse and children	_____
	Trustee may distribute income to spouse, children, or other or accumulate	_____

Spouses right to withdraw

	Trust B assets	_____
	Limited Standards	_____
	Greater of $5,000 or 5%	_____

Trustee may distribute Trust B Assets

	To spouse	_____
	To children	_____
	To others	_____

Limited Power of Appointment

	During spouse's lifetime	_____
	By will at spouse's death	_____

Other Provisions _____

FIGURE A.22 *Continued*

REVOCABLE TRUST

NAME:

UPON DEATH OF GRANTOR AND SPOUSE

All trust assets (A and B) and usually spouse's assets combine
for the benefit of the children and/or others and are:

ART. & PAR.

Maintained in a single fund until the
youngest child attains age _____
at which time the fund is divided into
equal shares

_____

Immediately divided into equal shares

_____

**After division but before children have
withdrawal rights:**

All income to children

_____

Trustee may distribute income
or accumulate

_____

Trustee may distribute assets

_____

Child's share withdrawal rights:

At age _____

_____

At age _____

_____

Balance at age _____

_____

MISCELLANEOUS PROVISIONS

Beneficiary's right to change trustee

_____

Simultaneous death clause

_____

Charitable distribution to: _____

_____

Generation Skipping Trust

_____

Ultimate Distribution Clause

_____

Spendthrift Clause

_____

FIGURE A.22 *Continued*

Estate Planning

TESTAMENTARY TRUST

GRANTOR:

TRUSTEE(S):

SUCCESSOR TRUSTEE(S):

DATE:

UPON DEATH OF TESTATOR AND SPOUSE

**All trust assets (A and B) and usually spouse's
assets combine for the benefit of the children
and/or others and are:**

ART. & PAR.

Maintained in a single fund until the
youngest child attains age _____
at which time the fund is divided into
equal shares

_____

Immediately divided into equal shares

_____

**After division but before children have
withdrawal rights:**

All income to children

_____

Trustee may distribute income
or accumulate

_____

Trustee may distribute assets

_____

Child's share withdrawal rights:

At age _____

_____

At age _____

_____

Balance at age _____

_____

MISCELLANEOUS PROVISIONS

Beneficiary's right to change trustee

_____

Simultaneous death clause

_____

Charitable distribution to: _____

_____

Generation Skipping Trust

_____

Ultimate Distribution Clause

_____

Spendthrift Clause

_____

FIGURE A.23 Testamentary Trust

Durable Power of Attorney—H

Name
Date
Attorney
Agent
Successor Agent
Provisions

FIGURE A.24 Durable Power of Attorney—Husband

Durable Power Of Attorney—W

Name
Date
Attorney
Agent
Successor Agent
Provisions

FIGURE A.25 Durable Power of Attorney—Wife

Health Care Proxy—H

Name Date Health Care Provisions

FIGURE A.26 Health Care Proxy—Husband

Health Care Proxy—W

Name Date Health Care Provisions

FIGURE A.27 Health Care Proxy—Wife

Health & Disability Insurance Planning

	Man		Woman		Documents
	Yes	No	Yes	No	Enclosed

1. Are you covered under a medical/dental expense reimbursement agreement with any corporation or other employer?

2. Are you covered under a wage continuation agreement with any corporation or other employer?

3. Do you have disability insurance?

4. In the event of your disability, is there an arrangement for the disposition of your business?

5. Do you have business overhead insurance?

6. Have you made any other provision to support you in the event of your disability? If so, give details.

7. Have you or your spouse smoked a cigarette in the last 12 months?

8. Do you, or any members of your family, have special health considerations that you know of, which could possibly result in declination of or exclusion on a life, health, , or disability insurance policy? If so, please provide details.

Name   Specific Impairment

	Man		Woman	
	Yes	No	Yes	No

Have you ever been declined for health or life insurance?

Have exclusions?

Been rated?

Prognosis:

	Man	Woman

9. In the event of your disability,

    A. How much income per month (before taxes) would the family require?

    B. How much income per month (before taxes) would your spouse be able to provide?
    For how long?

    C. Would you continue to live in your present home?

FIGURE A.28 Health and Disability Insurance Planning

Estate Planning

(Please enclose copies of wills, trust agreements, instruments creating powers of appointment, business agreements, and any other supporting documentation.)

	Man		Woman		Documents
	Yes	No	Yes	No	Enclosed
1. Do you have a will?					
2. Do you have a trust?					
3. Have you ever made substantial gifts?					
Have you filed a federal gift tax return?					
4. Do you have plans for gifts or support to your relatives or others during your lifetime? If so, give details					
At your death? if so, give details					
5. Are you named as executor, alternate executor, guardian, or trustee in anyone's will or trust? (other than spouse's)					
6. Do you have a business agreement that governs the position of the interest of any associate who dies?					
7. In the event of your death, would you prefer the business to continue?					
8. Have you completed any other estate planning?					
9. Would you like to provide for any charities? If yes, which ones? How much? In what manner?					
10. Do you have a durable power of attorney?					
11. Have you ever lived while married in a community property state? They are: Arizona, California, Idaho, Louisiana, Nevada, New Mexico, Texas, Washington, and Wisconsin.					

FIGURE A.29 Estate Planning

12. Do you expect an inheritance?
    Amount
    From whom?
    Within 10 years?
    Within 20 years?
    Other, please specify

Man	Woman

13. In the event of your death,

    (a) How much income per month (before
        taxes) would the family require?

    (b) For how long would this income be required?
        For spouse's life
        Other (please specify number of years)

    (c) How much income per month (before taxes)
        would your spouse be able to provide?
        For how long?

    (d) Would the family continue to live in their
        present home?

    (e) Should a college fund be provided?

    (f) Are there any assets that should not be sold
        at your death? If so, provide details

FIGURE A.29 *Continued*

Retirement Planning

(Please enclose copies of plan documents, joinder agreements, summary plan descriptions, most recent participant or allocation statements, and any other supporting documentation.)

	Man		Woman		Documents
	Yes	No	Yes	No	Enclosed
1. Do you have an Individual Retirement Account (IRA)?					
2. Do you have a Keogh (HR-10) Plan?					
3. Are you a participant in a State Teachers or Public Employees Retirement System?					
4. Do you have an interest in a retirement plan from a previous employment?					
5. Do you have a Tax-Sheltered Annuity Plan 403(b)?					
6. Are you a participant in a Defined Benefit Pension Plan?					
7. Are you a participant in a Money Purchase Pension Plan?					
8. Are you a participant in a Profit Sharing Plan?					
9. Do you have a Deferred Compensation Plan or a salary continuation agreement with your employer?					
10. Do you have an employment agreement with your employer?					
11. Are you eligible for retirement benefits from any other source?					
12. Do you have a Single Premium Deferred Annuity or Investment Annuity?					

FIGURE A.30 Retirement Planning

141

13. BUSINESS BACKGROUND: Furnish below a complete consecutive statement of all business experience and employment beyond formal school. List the most recent position first. Continue on back of page if additional space is needed.

Name of Firm or Business	Kind of Business	Position	Beginning Date		Ending Date	
			Month	Year	Month	Year

Man	Woman

14. At what age to you wish to retire?

How much income will you want per month (before taxes) in today's dollars?

Do you anticipate a slow-down (transition) period prior to retirement?

At what age will you slow down?

What percent of the stated retirement goal above will you be able to earn during the slow-down period?

Do you plan on selling your business at your retirement?

15. Are you planning to add a partner or associate?

16. Do you plan to work for compensation on a part-time basis after retirement?

17. Are you a trustee for any retirement plans?

18. Do you have a business agreement that governs the disposition of the interest of any associate who quits or retires?

19. Does the family have the ability to continue your business?

FIGURE A.30 *Continued*

Education / Dependent Planning

Names of Children	1	2	3	4	5	6
1. Child's grade level in fall at (year) (or if child is not yet in school, year child will start first grade.)						
2. Is child currently in private primary, private secondary, college, or graduate school?						
3. If yes to #2, what is the current annual cost?						
4. Will child attend private primary or secondary school in the future?						
5. If yes to #4, which grades?						
6. Will child attend college?						
7. If yes to #6, how many years?						
8. If yes to #6, what percentage of education costs will you pay?						
9. If yes to #6, what type* of institution will child attend?						
10. Will child attend graduate school?						
11. If yes to #10, how many years?						
12. If yes to #10, what percentage of graduate education casts will you pay?						
13. If yes to #10, what type of institution will child attend?						

*State supported or private; out-of-state or in-state; or vocational.

Comments:

FIGURE A.31 Education/Dependent Planning

(Enclose copies of trust agreements, most recent trust tax return,
and any other supporting documentation.)

	Man		Woman		Documents
	Yes	No	Yes	No	Enclosed
1. Have you established an education trust for your children?					
2. Are any children employed part-time in your business?					
3. Have you made interest-free loans to your children?					
4. Have you begun any investment or savings programs for your children's education?					

5. If yes to #4, please list:

Asset	Value

Do you plan to pay for a child's wedding, bar mitzvah, etc.?

If yes, what occasion? _____

When?

How much? ($)

For which child?

OTHER DEPENDENTS

Are you supporting any other person?

If so, whom?

What is the cost?

FIGURE A.31 *Continued*

Income Planning

(Enclose copies of two most recent consecutive paycheck stubs and personal federal tax returns, Form 1040, for the three most recent years.)

Man	Woman

1. Please indicate current annual gross salary. (If from more than one source, list each source separately.)

2. If self-employed (i.e., not incorporated and not an employee), please indicate expected net income from self-employment for current year.

3. Expected bonus for current year.

4. Expected commissions for current year.

5. If you are currently receiving Social Security benefits, please indicate amount.

6. If you are currently receiving other types of retirement income, please indicate source and amount.

Source

Amount

Additional Goal and/or Factors to be Considered in Planning:

FIGURE A.32 Income Planning

Client Name					
Address					
City					

Financial Planning Invoice
9/7/00

BUSINESS AND INVESTMENT PLANNING FOR THE PERIOD :
11/1/99　　　　　　through　　　　　　10/30/00

Earned Income:	$	800,000	1.00%		$	8,000
Investments:	$	500,000				
First half-million			500,000	0.75%	$	3,750
Next half-million			0	0.50%	$	-
Over a million			0	0.25%	$	-
TOTAL CALCULATED FEE:					$	11,750
ACTUAL FEE:					$	11,750

Date Due	Amount Due	Check Number	Amount Paid		Balance
11/1/99	$ 5,875	$	-	$	5,875
2/1/00	$ 2,938	$	-	$	8,813
5/2/00	$ 2,938	$	-	$	11,750

If you would like a current copy of my ADV, please let me know so I can send it to you.

John E. Sestina – 7677 Tamarisk Court – Dublin, OH 43016
(614) 798-1742

FIGURE A.33 Fee Calculation

John E. Sestina and Company

September 7, 2000

Client Name
Address
City

Dear (Name of Client),

It is time to renew our financial planning agreement. Enclosed you will find the fee calculation. Please review for your approval. If you have any questions please call. Otherwise, I am looking forward to our next meeting on   (Date of Meeting).

If you would like a current copy of my ADV, please let me know so I can send it to you.

Keep up the good work.

Sincerely yours,

John E. Sestina, CFP, ChFC, MSFS

FIGURE A.33 *Continued*

Second Set of Forms Needed

MATERIALS AND DATA REQUIRED

A. Materials Needed

   1. Calculator

   2. Manila Folders

   3. Accordion File

B. Data Required (Folder Headings)

   1. Cash Equivalents (Checking and Savings Accounts)

   2. Stocks

   3. Bonds

   4. Oil, Gas, Mineral Investments or Rights

   5. Real Estate
      Residence
      Investment
      REIT (Real Estate Investment Trust)

   6. Receivables

   7. Business Interests
      Employment Agreement
      Medical/Dental Agreement
      Buy/Sell Agreement
      Partnership Agreements
      Corporate Tax Returns (1120)

   8. Liabilities
      Mortgages
      Installment Loans
      Credit Cards
      Leases

   9. Life Insurance

  10. Health and Accident Insurance
      Hospitalization/Major Medical
      Expense Reimbursement
      Disability

  11. General Insurance
      Homeowners/PCP (Property Comprehensive Policy)
      Automobile
      Office

FIGURE B.1 Materials and Data Required

Professional Liability
Umbrella
Fidelity
Marine

12. Estate Planning
Wills
Trusts
Powers of Attorney

13. Retirement Planning
Defined-Contribution Pension (Also Called "Money Purchase")
Defined-Benefit Pension
Profit Sharing
Keogh
IRA
401(k)
Public Employee Retirement System
State Teacher Retirement System

14. Education Planning

15. Income Planning
Personal Tax Returns (1040)

16. Miscellaneous

<hr />

FIGURE B.1 *Continued*

Financial Planning Services Agreement

Set forth below is the basis upon which John E. Sestina and Company will furnish financial planning services to the Client.

1. All information and advice furnished by either party to the other, including their respective agents and employees, shall be treated as confidential and shall not be disclosed to third parties except as required by law and with mutual consent and foreknowledge.

2. John E. Sestina and Company will review, in detail, the Client's current financial position including assets, liabilities, cash management, employee benefits, insurance, estate plan, and other detailed factors pertaining to Client's financial position, individual goals, and future objectives.

3. In order to enable John E. Sestina and Company to make the above review, the Client will furnish John E. Sestina and Company with a copy of such documents or other information as John E. Sestina and Company may reasonably request, all of which will be held in confidence.

4. After collection of all data and documents, John E. Sestina and Company will process and coordinate all information gathered, assimilate all aspects pertaining to Client's case, and project known conditions into future assumptions, and will make recommendations in a written, concise, personalized financial plan aimed at improving asset utilization, capital accumulation, and goal achievement.

5. John E. Sestina and Company will make a supplemental analysis in each subsequent year this agreement is renewed and will update, in writing, those recommendations as necessary in relation to conditions existing at the time of each annual review.

6. The contract for these services shall be one year beginning with the date this agreement is accepted by John E. Sestina and Company. This contract will not be assigned without the consent of the Client.

7. Fees charged by John E. Sestina and Company are for financial and investment advisory services. John E. Sestina and Company fees are distinguished from supplementary legal, investment, insurance, or accounting fees which might be incurred by Client as a result of implementing recommendations of Client's financial plan.

   Examples of services *not* performed by John E. Sestina and Company are: income tax preparation, retirement plan accounting, retirement plan administration, preparation of legal documents, etc.

8. From time to time we give advice, which should be reviewed by Client's accountant and/or attorney. It is agreed and understood that in connection with recommendations made with respect to Client, accounting and legal fees and other expenses may, from time to time, be incurred. In the event the recom-

---

FIGURE B.2 Financial Planning Services Agreement

mendation of John E. Sestina and Company is taken by the Client with respect to the purchase, sale, or retention of any security or property of the Client, the Client will pay such fees and expenses so incurred.

9. It is agreed and understood that John E. Sestina and Company will at no time take possession of, or exercise discretion over, any of the Client's investments or property. While we will make recommendations and give advice concerning the purchase, sale, or retention of Client's securities or property, the final decision to implement such a recommendation will always be made by the Client.

10. It is agreed and understood that John E. Sestina and Company in no event will accept or receive fees, commissions, or other remuneration or compensation of whatever kind or description from advisors, originators, sponsors, syndicators, or distributors of investments recommended to the Clients of John E. Sestina and Company.

11. From time to time John E. Sestina and Company may effect transactions for its own account in investments recommended for purchase or sale by John E. Sestina and Company to Client. Any such purchase or sale by John E. Sestina and Company will be on terms identical with that recommended to Clients, and that in the case of a sale of an investment, John E. Sestina and Company will notify Client of its intention to dispose of such investment. If Client wishes to dispose of such investment, such interest will be sold if possible at the same time and on the same terms as that being sold by John E. Sestina and Company. It is agreed that in the event both the Client's and John E. Sestina and Company interests cannot all be sold, the Client's interest to the extent possible will be sold first.

12. Client understands that any time within five (5) business days after the date of entering into this agreement with John E. Sestina and Company, Client may terminate this agreement without penalty and will receive a complete refund of any fees paid to John E. Sestina and Company.

13. On an annual basis, upon Client's written request, John E. Sestina and Company will provide Client with a copy of John E. Sestina and Company Form ADV or such other brochure as John E. Sestina and Company may prepare.

FIGURE B.2 *Continued*

John E. Sestina and Company

Date

Client Name
Address

Dear

It was a pleasure meeting with you and discussing our services. We are pleased that you have chosen John E. Sestina and Company to assist you with your financial planning. Thank you for taking the time to complete the information on the questionnaire; we recognize that this was a time-consuming job. A personal financial analyst will review the information you have provided and will contact you for further data.

As your financial planners, our analysis and recommendations will focus on the goals and objectives which you have given us and which we will develop together. We look forward to this opportunity.

Enclosed is our invoice as calculated during our first meeting. An authorization letter is also enclosed which we would like you to sign and return with your deposit check. An envelope is enclosed for your convenience.

Our office manager, Kathy Goodrich, will call to schedule your first planning meeting. We will require two to three hours for this first meeting.

Please call with any questions you have during this analysis period. Thank you for the opportunity to be of service.

Cordially,

John E. Sestina
Enclosures

FIGURE B.3 Letter of Confirmation

SESTINA, BUDROS & RUHLIN, INC.

3726-J OLENTANGY RIVER ROAD
COLUMBUS, OHIO 43214

(614) 457-8200

May 2, 1991

Mr. & Mrs. Harry Sample
1000 Happy Lane
Columbus, OH

===

BUSINESS TAX AND INVESTMENT PLANNING for the PERIOD

6-1-91 through 5-31-92

===

Financial Advisory Fee:

$ _____   X   _____ % = $_____

Investment Management Fee:

$ _____   X   _____ % = $_____

TOTAL CALCULATED FEE $_____

TOTAL ANNUAL FEE $_____

Payment No. 1   Deposit Due Now $_____

Payment No. 2   Due in 3 Months $_____

Payment No. 3   Due in 6 Months $_____

PLEASE MAKE YOUR CHECK PAYABLE TO SESTINA, BUDROS & RUHLIN, INC.

FIGURE B.4 Sample Invoice

Sample Worksheets

CASH FLOW WORKSHEET

Sample	Mar	Apr	May	Jun	Jul	Aug
1 Cash available	5,000					
Income						
2 Salary	6,000	6,000	6,000	6,000	6,000	6,000
3 Self-employment net income						
4 Investment income						
5 Total Income	6,000	6,000	6,000	6,000	6,000	6,000
6 Total Cash	11,000	6,000	6,000	6,000	6,000	6,000
Expenses						
7 Taxes—personal property	0	0	0	0	0	0
8 Taxes—real estate	0	0	0	0	0	0
9 Home maintenance	200	200	200	200	200	200
10 Food	100	100	100	100	100	100
11 Household expenses	500	500	500	500	500	500
12 Medical/dental	150	50	250	150	50	50
13 Clothes	700	500	500	500	500	1,500
14 Charitable contributions	200	200	200	200	200	200
15 Auto—gas/repairs	200	200	200	200	200	200
16 Home mortgage #1	1,400	1,400	1,400	1,400	1,400	1,400
17 Telephone—home	100	100	100	100	100	100
18 Electric—home	400	200	200	200	200	200
19 Water—home	65	65	150	150	150	100
20 Cable—home	48	48	48	48	48	48
21 Business expense	400	400	100	400	100	100
22 Education	0	0	0	0	0	0
23 Insurance—life	0	1,500	0	0	1,500	0
24 Insurance—home	0	0	0	0	0	0
25 Insurance—car	200	200	200	200	200	200
26 Insurance—personal umbrella	0	0	0	0	0	0
27 Gifts	50	50	50	50	50	50
28 Vacations	0	0	0	0	2,000	0
29 Miscellaneous	200	200	200	200	200	200
30 Lessons	245	245	245	0	0	0
31 Camp	0	1,000	0	0	0	0
32 Bank #1	239	239	239	239	239	239
33 Bank #2	300	300	300	300	300	300
34 Bank #3	150	150	150	150	150	150
35 Bank #4	200	200	200	200	200	200
36 Total Expenses	6,047	8,047	5,532	5,487	8,587	6,037
37 Net Income	4,953	(2,047)	468	513	(2,587)	(37)
38 Cumulative Surplus	4,953	2,906	3,374	3,887	1,300	1,263

FIGURE C.1 Cash Flow Worksheet

Sep	Oct	Nov	Dec	Jan	Feb	Totals	
						5,000	1
6,000	6,000	6,000	6,000	6,000	6,000	72,000	2
							3
							4
6,000	6,000	6,000	6,000	6,000	6,000	72,000	5
6,000	6,000	6,000	6,000	6,000	6,000	77,000	6
0	0	0	3,000	0	0	3,000	7
0	0	0	4,000	0	0	4,000	8
200	200	200	200	200	200	2,400	9
100	100	100	100	100	100	1,200	10
500	500	500	500	500	500	6,200	11
150	50	50	150	50	50	1,200	12
500	500	1,500	500	500	500	8,200	13
200	200	200	200	200	200	2,400	14
200	200	200	200	200	200	2,400	15
1,400	1,400	1,400	1,400	1,400	1,400	16,800	16
100	100	100	100	100	100	1,200	17
250	300	400	400	500	400	3,650	18
100	100	65	65	65	65	1,140	19
48	48	48	48	48	48	576	20
400	100	100	400	100	100	2,700	21
0	0	0	0	0	0	0	22
0	1,500	0	0	1,500	0	6,000	23
0	0	0	0	0	0	0	24
200	200	200	200	200	200	2,400	25
0	0	0	0	0	0	0	26
50	50	50	50	50	50	600	27
0	0	0	0	0	1,500	3,500	28
200	200	200	200	200	200	2,400	29
245	245	245	245	245	245	2,205	30
0	0	0	0	0	0	1,000	31
239	239	239	239	239	239	2,868	32
300	300	300	300	300	300	3,600	33
150	150	150	150	150	150	1,800	34
200	200	200	200	200	200	2,400	35
5,732	6,882	6,447	12,847	7,047	6,947	85,839	36
268	(882)	(447)	(6,847)	(1,047)	(947)	(8,639)	37
1,531	649	202	(6,645)	(7,692)	(8,639)		38

FIGURE C.1 *Continued*

DISABILITY PLANNING

CLIENT

Present Age	45
Age Death Assumed	72
Investment Earnings	8%
Inflation Rate	4%
Present Investments	243,372
Income Goal	90,000
Spouse Can Provide	72,000
Social Security	8,640
PRESENT INSURANCE	36,000
COLA Rider Percentage	5%

Yr	Age	Date	Present Invest	Spouse Income	Disability Insurance	Social Security	Pension Income	Income Goal	Funds Remaining	Interest
1	45	2000	243,372	72,000	36,000	8,640	0	90,000	270,012	21,601
2	46	2001	291,613	74,880	37,800	8,986	0	93,600	319,679	25,574
3	47	2002	345,253	77,875	39,690	9,345	0	97,344	374,819	29,986
4	48	2003	404,805	80,990	41,675	9,719	0	101,238	435,950	34,876
5	49	2004	470,826	84,230	43,758	10,108	0	105,287	503,635	40,291
6	50	2005	543,926	87,599	45,946	10,512	0	109,499	578,484	46,279
7	51	2006	624,762	91,103	48,243	10,932	0	113,879	661,163	52,893
8	52	2007	714,056	94,747	50,656	11,370	0	118,434	752,394	60,192
9	53	2008	812,586	98,537	53,188	11,824	0	123,171	852,964	68,237
10	54	2009	921,201	102,478	55,848	12,297	0	128,098	963,727	77,098
11	55	2010	1,040,825	106,578	58,640	12,789	0	133,222	1,085,610	86,849
12	56	2011	1,172,459	110,841	61,572	13,301	0	138,551	1,219,622	97,570
13	57	2012	1,317,192	115,274	64,651	13,833	0	144,093	1,366,857	109,349
14	58	2013	1,476,205	119,885	67,883	14,386	0	149,857	1,528,504	122,280
15	59	2014	1,650,784	124,681	71,278	14,962	0	155,851	1,705,853	136,468
16	60	2015	1,842,321	129,668	74,841	15,560	0	162,085	1,900,306	152,024
17	61	2016	2,052,330	134,855	78,583	16,183	0	168,568	2,113,383	169,071
18	62	2017	2,282,453	140,249	82,513	16,830	0	175,311	2,346,734	187,739
19	63	2018	2,534,472	145,859	86,638	17,503	0	182,323	2,602,149	208,172
20	64	2019	2,810,321	151,693	90,970	18,203	0	189,616	2,881,571	230,526
21	65	2020	3,112,097	157,761	95,519	18,931	0	197,201	3,187,106	254,969
22	66	2021	3,442,075	164,071	100,295	19,689	0	205,089	3,521,040	281,683
23	67	2022	3,802,724	170,634	105,309	20,476	0	213,293	3,885,851	310,868
24	68	2023	4,196,719	177,460	110,575	21,295	0	221,824	4,284,224	342,738
25	69	2024	4,626,962	184,558	116,104	22,147	0	230,697	4,719,073	377,526
26	70	2025	5,096,598	191,940	121,909	23,033	0	239,925	5,193,555	415,484
27	71	2026	5,609,039	199,618	128,004	23,954	0	249,522	5,711,093	456,887
28	72	2027	6,167,981	207,603	134,404	24,912	0	259,503	6,275,397	502,032
29	73	2028	6,777,429	215,907	141,125	25,909	0	269,883	6,890,485	551,239
30	74	2029	7,441,724	224,543	148,181	26,945	0	280,679	7,560,715	604,857
31	75	2030	8,165,572	233,525	155,590	28,023	0	291,906	8,290,803	663,264

FIGURE C.2 Disability Planning

Education Planning

9/20/00

CHILD'S FIRST AND LAST NAMES	Child 1	Child 2	Child 3	
INFLATION RATE for COLLEGE COSTS		8.00%		ENDING
CURRENT PORTFOLIO INVESTMENT RETURN		10.00%		ACCOUNT
RISK-FREE INVESTMENT RETURN		7.00%		BALANCE:
NEED TO SAVE EACH YEAR		10,890		147
% SAVINGS INCREASE PER YEAR		0.00%		
AGE	6	4	2	
PRESENT INVESTMENTS	0	0	0	
Add'l savings to Sept.	0	0	0	
UNDER-GRADUATE:				
Year of Entry	2012	2014	2016	
# Years to Attend	4	4	4	
Today's Cost	10,000	10,000	10,000	
Percent to Pay	100%	100%	100%	
GRADUATE:				
Year of Entry	0	0	0	
# Years to Attend	4	4	4	
Today's Cost	0	0	0	
Percent to Pay	100%	100%	100%	

FIGURE C.3 Education Planning

161

P.V. OF TOTAL COSTS 98,169

LUMP-SUM NEEDED TODAY 98,169

	Year	98,169	98,169		Beg. Balance	Save Per Yr	Need	Remainder	Earnings	End. Balance
0	Beginning Sept., 2000	0	0	0	0	10,890	0	10,890	1,089	11,979
1	2001	0	0	0	11,979	10,890	0	22,869	2,287	25,156
2	2002	0	0	0	25,156	10,890	0	36,046	3,605	39,650
3	2003	0	0	0	39,650	10,890	0	50,540	5,054	55,595
4	2004	0	0	0	55,595	10,890	0	66,485	6,648	73,133
5	2005	0	0	0	73,133	10,890	0	84,023	8,402	92,425
6	2006	0	0	0	92,425	10,890	0	103,315	10,332	113,647
7	2007	0	0	0	113,647	10,890	0	124,537	12,454	136,991
8	2008	0	0	0	136,991	10,890	0	147,881	14,788	162,669
9	2009	0	0	0	162,669	10,890	0	173,559	17,356	190,914
10	2010	0	0	0	190,914	10,890	0	201,804	14,126	215,931
11	2011	0	0	0	215,931	10,890	0	226,821	15,877	242,698
12	2012	25,182	0	0	242,698	10,890	25,182	228,406	15,988	244,395
13	2013	27,196	0	0	244,395	10,890	27,196	228,089	15,966	244,055
14	2014	29,372	29,372	0	244,055	10,890	58,744	196,201	13,734	209,935
15	2015	31,722	31,722	0	209,935	10,890	63,443	157,382	11,017	168,398
16	2016	0	34,259	34,259	168,398	10,890	68,519	110,770	7,754	118,523
17	2017	0	37,000	37,000	118,523	10,890	74,000	55,413	3,879	59,292
18	2018	0	0	39,960	59,292	10,890	39,960	30,222	2,116	32,337
19	2019	0	0	43,157	32,337	10,890	43,157	70	5	75
20	2020	0	0	0	75	0	0	75	8	83
21	2021	0	0	0	83	0	0	83	8	91
22	2022	0	0	0	91	0	0	91	9	100
23	2023	0	0	0	100	0	0	100	10	110
24	2024	0	0	0	110	0	0	110	11	121
25	2025	0	0	0	121	0	0	121	12	133
26	2026	0	0	0	133	0	0	133	13	147
27	2027	0	0	0	147	0	0	147	15	161
	TOTAL	113,472	132,353	154,377						

FIGURE C.3 *Continued*

Retirement Planning

CLIENT

Present Age	35	
Retirement Age	65	
Investment Earnings	8.00%	
Tax Bracket	30.00%	
After-Tax Earnings	5.60%	
Inflation Rate	4.00%	
Present Investments	0	
Slowdown Income Goal	0	
Retirement Income Goal	23,000	16,100 After-Tax Income
Social Security	0	
Age Receives Soc Security	62	Balance at Age:
Investment Required	25,000 1,844,755	85
Pre-Tax Investment Needed	35,714 103,306	85

Yr	Age	Date	Present Invest	Annual Invest	Social Security	H - Pension Income	W - Inherit./ Pension Income	Bus. Sale	Retire Goal	Funds Remaining	Earnings
1	35	2000	0	25,000	0	0	0	0	0	25,000	1,400
2	36	2001	26,400	25,000	0	0	0	0	0	51,400	2,878
3	37	2002	54,278	25,000	0	0	0	0	0	79,278	4,440
4	38	2003	83,718	25,000	0	0	0	0	0	108,718	6,088
5	39	2004	114,806	25,000	0	0	0	0	0	139,806	7,829
6	40	2005	147,635	25,000	0	0	0	0	0	172,635	9,668
7	41	2006	182,303	25,000	0	0	0	0	0	207,303	11,609
8	42	2007	218,912	25,000	0	0	0	0	0	243,912	13,659
9	43	2008	257,571	25,000	0	0	0	0	0	282,571	15,824
10	44	2009	298,395	25,000	0	0	0	0	0	323,395	18,110
11	45	2010	341,505	25,000	0	0	0	0	0	366,505	20,524
12	46	2011	387,029	25,000	0	0	0	0	0	412,029	23,074
13	47	2012	435,103	25,000	0	0	0	0	0	460,103	25,766
14	48	2013	485,869	25,000	0	0	0	0	0	510,869	28,609
15	49	2014	539,477	25,000	0	0	0	0	0	564,477	31,611
16	50	2015	596,088	25,000	0	0	0	0	0	621,088	34,781
17	51	2016	655,869	25,000	0	0	0	0	0	680,869	38,129
18	52	2017	718,998	25,000	0	0	0	0	0	743,998	41,664
19	53	2018	785,662	25,000	0	0	0	0	0	810,662	45,397
20	54	2019	856,059	25,000	0	0	0	0	0	881,059	49,339
21	55	2020	930,398	25,000	0	0	0	0	0	955,398	53,502
22	56	2021	1,008,900	25,000	0	0	0	0	0	1,033,900	57,898
23	57	2022	1,091,799	25,000	0	0	0	0	0	1,116,799	62,541
24	58	2023	1,179,339	25,000	0	0	0	0	0	1,204,339	67,443
25	59	2024	1,271,782	25,000	0	0	0	0	0	1,296,782	72,620
26	60	2025	1,369,402	25,000	0	0	0	0	0	1,394,402	78,087
27	61	2026	1,472,489	25,000	0	0	0	0	0	1,497,489	83,859
28	62	2027	1,581,348	25,000	0	0	0	0	0	1,606,348	89,955
29	63	2028	1,696,304	25,000	0	0	0	0	0	1,721,304	96,393

FIGURE C.4 Retirement Planning

30	64	2029	1,817,697	25,000	0	0	0	0	0	1,842,697	103,191
31	65	2030	1,945,888	25,000	0	0	0	0	74,598	1,896,289	106,192
32	66	2031	2,002,482	0	0	0	0	0	77,582	1,924,900	107,794
33	67	2032	2,032,694	0	0	0	0	0	80,685	1,952,009	109,312
34	68	2033	2,061,321	0	0	0	0	0	83,913	1,977,408	110,735
35	69	2034	2,088,143	0	0	0	0	0	87,269	2,000,874	112,049
36	70	2035	2,112,923	0	0	0	0	0	90,760	2,022,163	113,241
37	71	2036	2,135,404	0	0	0	0	0	94,390	2,041,013	114,297
38	72	2037	2,155,310	0	0	0	0	0	98,166	2,057,144	115,200
39	73	2038	2,172,344	0	0	0	0	0	102,093	2,070,251	115,934
40	74	2039	2,186,186	0	0	0	0	0	106,176	2,080,009	116,481
41	75	2040	2,196,490	0	0	0	0	0	110,423	2,086,066	116,820
42	76	2041	2,202,886	0	0	0	0	0	114,840	2,088,045	116,931
43	77	2042	2,204,976	0	0	0	0	0	119,434	2,085,542	116,790
44	78	2043	2,202,332	0	0	0	0	0	124,211	2,078,121	116,375
45	79	2044	2,194,496	0	0	0	0	0	129,180	2,065,316	115,658
46	80	2045	2,180,974	0	0	0	0	0	134,347	2,046,626	114,611
47	81	2046	2,161,238	0	0	0	0	0	139,721	2,021,517	113,205
48	82	2047	2,134,722	0	0	0	0	0	145,310	1,989,412	111,407
49	83	2048	2,100,819	0	0	0	0	0	151,122	1,949,697	109,183
50	84	2049	2,058,880	0	0	0	0	0	157,167	1,901,713	106,496
51	85	2050	2,008,209	0	0	0	0	0	163,454	1,844,755	103,306
52	86	2051	1,948,061	0	0	0	0	0	169,992	1,778,069	99,572
53	87	2052	1,877,641	0	0	0	0	0	176,792	1,700,850	95,248
54	88	2053	1,796,097	0	0	0	0	0	183,863	1,612,234	90,285
55	89	2054	1,702,519	0	0	0	0	0	191,218	1,511,301	84,633
56	90	2055	1,595,934	0	0	0	0	0	198,866	1,397,068	78,236

FIGURE C.4 *Continued*

Estate Planning

CLIENT

Present Age of Survivor	83
Age Benefit Terminates	95
Inflation Rate	4%
Investment Rate	8%
Income Goal	12,000
Family Share	1,300,100
Education Fund	0
Family Income Needs	219,932
Surplus/(Deficit)	1,080,168

Yr	Date	Age	Goal Desired	Social Security	Other Income	Deficit
1	2000	83	12,000	0	0	12,000
2	2001	84	12,480	0	0	12,480
3	2002	85	12,979	0	0	12,979
4	2003	86	13,498	0	0	13,498
5	2004	87	14,038	0	0	14,038
6	2005	88	14,600	0	0	14,600
7	2006	89	15,184	0	0	15,184
8	2007	90	15,791	0	0	15,791
9	2008	91	16,423	0	0	16,423
10	2009	92	17,080	0	0	17,080
11	2010	93	17,763	0	0	17,763
12	2011	94	18,473	0	0	18,473
13	2012	95	19,212	0	0	19,212
14	2013	96	19,981	0	0	19,981
15	2014	97	20,780	0	0	20,780
16	2015	98	21,611	0	0	21,611
17	2016	99	22,476	0	0	22,476
18	2017	100	23,375	0	0	23,375
19	2018	101	24,310	0	0	24,310
20	2019	102	25,282	0	0	25,282
21	2020	103	26,293	0	0	26,293
22	2021	104	27,345	0	0	27,345
23	2022	105	28,439	0	0	28,439
24	2023	106	29,577	0	0	29,577
25	2024	107	30,760	0	0	30,760
26	2025	108	31,990	0	0	31,990
27	2026	109	33,270	0	0	33,270
28	2027	110	34,600	0	0	34,600
29	2028	111	35,984	0	0	35,984
30	2029	112	37,424	0	0	37,424
31	2030	113	38,921	0	0	38,921
32	2031	114	40,478	0	0	40,478
33	2032	115	42,097	0	0	42,097
34	2033	116	43,781	0	0	43,781
35	2034	117	45,532	0	0	45,532

FIGURE C.5 Estate Planning

Implementation Checklist

IMPLEMENTATION CHECKLIST
for the Client as of 6/23/00 10:31 A.M.

I. Important Information

   A. Complete a household inventory.

   B. Update household inventory.

   C. Have broker send duplicate confirmations and statements to John E. Sestina and Company.

   D. Obtain passports for all family members.

   E. Consider prenuptial agreement.

II. Income Analysis

   A. Meet with accountant in _____ to project income taxes.

   B. Complete projected cash flow worksheet.

   C. Save ____ % of all you earn.

   D. Pay cash for everything.

   E. Keep records of all financial transactions.

   F. Increase/decrease your salary by $_____ a year.

   G. Establish deferred compensation plan with _____ for $____ per year.

   H. Please send copies of 1999 federal and state tax returns when completed.

   I. Consider establishing a charitable remainder trust.

   J. Consider a foundation for charitable giving.

   K. Last year you made cash contributions to charities of $_____. Consider gifting appreciated securities in lieu of cash for additional tax savings.

   L. _____ should earn $____ from the corporation in order to qualify for the Ohio joint filing credit and fund a nondeductible IRA.

   M. Establish cash flow budget.

III. Balance Sheet

   A. As of _____, your net worth increased ____% per year since _____.

   B. Your net worth increased ____% from _____ to _____.

FIGURE D.1 Implementation Checklist

IV. Asset/Liability Information

    A. Liability:

        1. Current interest rate is _____%.

        2. Deductible home mortgage interest.

        3. Deductible investment interest.

        4. Deductible passive activity interest.

        5. Nondeductible consumer loan interest.

        6. Obtain proposals from various lenders for a new fixed-rate 15-year mortgage.

        7. Refinance _____.

        8. Pay off _____.

        9. Borrow $_____ from your home equity line of credit/corporation to pay off this loan.

        10. Send John E. Sestina and Company a recent statement with the current balance for all liabilities.

        11. Loan status is as recommended.

    B. Request, in writing, lender's backup data when ARM payments are reset in _____.

    C. Pay credit card balance monthly.

    D. Make additional principal payments of $_____ each.

    E. Make payment of $_____ due _____.

V. Investments

    A. Prior to redemption of any investment account, determine if there is a surrender charge or redemption fee.

    B. Complete an investment profile and determine your cash reserve fund.

    C. You have determined that your investment portfolio should be divided into the following categories:

        1. $_____ Cash Reserve fund invested in _____.

        2. $_____ Short-Term/"Special Purpose" fund for _____ invested in _____.

        3 Long-Term Portfolio:

            a. % Fixed Income

                (1) % Domestic Fixed Income

                (2) % International Fixed Income

            b. % Equities

FIGURE D.1 *Continued*

    (3) % Large/Mid-Cap

    (4) % Small Company

    (5) % International

  c. % Real Estate

  d. % Gold/Precious Metals

  e. %

D. Cash Equivalents:

  1. Change ownership from joint to _____.

  2. Build/maintain cash reserve fund of $_____ in the _____.

  3. Transfer all excess cash to _____ money market account.

  4 When _____ CDs mature, transfer funds to _____ money market account.

  5. Redeem _____ CD's now and transfer funds to _____ money market account.

  6. Invest $_____ in _____ money market fund.

  7. Open a _____ money market fund. Invest $_____.

  8. Close the following accounts:

  9. Withdraw the following amounts from the following accounts:

E. Stocks:

  1. Change ownership from joint to _____.

  2. Transfer stocks to Charles Schwab & Co.

  3. Instruct brokers to furnish John E. Sestina and Company with detailed information on your present holdings, including:

    a. Date purchased

    b. Purchase price

    c. Interim sales (dates and amounts)

    d. Rate of return analysis

  4. Sell _____.

F. Bonds:

  1. Series EE bonds automatically mature after 40 years even if they are not cashed. Therefore, bonds purchased before 1955 will mature this year and the interest will be subject to taxation.

  2. Series E bonds issued in 1965 automatically mature in 30 years. Therefore those bonds will be subject to taxation in 1995.

  3. Change ownership from joint to _____.

  4. Invest $_____ in municipal/corporate bonds personally/in retirement plan.

  5. Purchase/sell Series EE/HH bonds.

FIGURE D.1 *Continued*

6. Sell _____.
7. Consider having a brokerage firm hold your bonds for valuation purposes.
8. Transfer bonds to Charles Schwab & Co.

G. Mutual Funds:
   1. Change ownership from joint to _____.
   2. Invest in the following funds:
   3. Sell the following funds:
   4. Withdraw the following amounts from the following funds:
      $
      $
      $
   5. Invest in the following funds over the next _____ months, utilizing a dollar-cost averaging plan:

   6. Transfer mutual funds to Charles Schwab & Co.
   7. Do not buy mutual funds in last quarter to avoid paying tax on dividend distributions.

H. Annuity:
   1. Invest $_____ in _____ annuity.
   2. Annuity:
      a. Send copy of prospectus for surrender charges and investment options.
      b. Consider surrender, realizing termination charge of _____.
      c. Change investment option from _____ to _____.
      d. Invest $_____ in the _____ investment annuity as follows:

I. Oil, Gas, Mineral, Precious Metals, Numismatics:
   1. Invest $_____ in gold American Eagles over the next _____ months, utilizing a dollar-cost averaging plan.
   2. Sell _____.

J. Real Estate:
   1. Residence:
      a. Keep a record of all home improvements.
      b. Have residence appraised.
      c. Consider selling residence.
      d. Purchase another residence for $_____.
      e. Gift _____ interest in residence from husband to wife.

FIGURE D.1 *Continued*

     f. Change ownership from joint to _____.

     g. Obtain a home equity line of credit.

     h. Determine the tax basis of your current residence, including any gains rolled over from previous residence sales.

  2. Property name:

     a. Have this property appraised.

     b. Consider selling this property.

     c. Purchase this property for $_____.

     d. Gift _____ from _____ to _____.

     e. Change ownership of _____ from joint to _____.

K. REIT:

  1. Sell _____.

L. Receivables:

  1. Receivable name:

     a. Draft note between _____ and _____.

     b. Loan $_____ to _____ at _____ % interest.

     c. Gift _____ note to _____.

     d. Initiate collection against _____.

     e. Initiate foreclosure against _____.

M. Venture Capital:

  1. Send prospectus/original documentation for _____ investment.

  2. Send _____ tax returns for review.

VI. Business Interests

A. Business Name:

  1. Set corporate year-end planning meeting with all your advisors prior to _____.

  2. Amend corporate employment agreement to include a short-term salary continuation provision.

  3. Amend partnership agreement.

  4. Establish _____ partnership.

  5. Execute lease for _____ between _____ and _____.

  6. Transfer all excess business cash to business money market.

  7. Complete Employee Census Data Sheet and return to John E. Sestina and Company.

  8. Furnish John E. Sestina and Company with a copy of most recent tax returns and/or financial statements for _____.

FIGURE D.1 *Continued*

9. Contribute equipment to trust for your children and lease to your corporation (see Dependent Planning).
10. Update corporate minutes book.
11. Establish Section 303 stock redemption plan.
12. Change fiscal year-end to _____.
13. Bond employees for fraud and embezzlement.
14. Establish group life insurance plan with $50,000 benefit for _____.
15. Change stock redemption agreement to cross purchase agreement.
16. Transfer ownership of corporate life insurance to _____.
17. Change from C corporation to S corporation.
18. If your spouse has no other income and performs services for the business, pay her/him annual compensation of $_____.
19. Premiums for personal life insurance policies which are paid by the corporation are taxable income to the policyholder and deductible by the corporation.

B. Establish a family partnership.

C. The first $5,000 of death benefits paid by an employer to an employee's surviving spouse is free from income tax.

VII. Property and Casualty Insurance

A. A review of your property and casualty coverage indicates no changes are necessary at this time.

B. Umbrella:
1. Add corporate/personal umbrella coverage of/to $_____.
2. Increase your underlying limits to required amount.
3. Renew your personal umbrella coverage no later than _____.

C. Homeowners:
1. Determine premium cost savings if deductibles are increased to $_____.
2. Increase deductible to $_____.
3. Check with your agent to assure the coverage is adequate to provide for replacement cost of dwelling.
4. Change coverage to form HO-3.
5. Add/increase scheduled property coverage.
6. Add contents replacement cost endorsement.
7. Renew your homeowners insurance no later than _____.

FIGURE D.1 *Continued*

8. Request list of all discounts available and apply for all those for which you are eligible.

D. Automobile:

1. Determine premium cost savings if deductibles are increased to $_____.

2. Add collision deductible of $_____.

3. Add comprehensive deductible of $_____.

4. Drop collision coverage.

5. Consult your agent to determine your coverage for nonlegal liability when renting an automobile.

6. Review your automobile lease with your agent to assure the policy will cover your remaining obligation under the lease.

7. Renew your automobile insurance no later than _____.

8. Request list of all discounts available and apply for all those for which you are eligible.

E. Office:

1. Add deductible of $_____.

2. Check with your agent to make sure your coverage will provide for replacement cost of building.

3. Add adequacy of contents coverage.

4. Add accounts receivable coverage.

5. Add loss of earnings coverage.

6. Add hired/nonowned auto coverage.

7. Check with your agent to be sure your contract provides adequate employee dishonesty coverage.

8. Request a list of all discounts available and apply for all those for which you are eligible.

9. Add employer's stop-gap coverage.

10. Have your insurance agent review your office lease to determine adequacy of coverage.

F. Professional Liability

1. Add corporate coverage of $_____.

G. Fidelity:

1. Add fidelity bond coverage of/to 10% of all retirement plan assets, including voluntary accounts.

H. Workers Compensation:

1. Apply for workers compensation coverage if you employ a housekeeper, baby-sitter, etc., in your home.

FIGURE D.1 *Continued*

2. You have indicated that you do not employ any household workers. Therefore, workers compensation insurance is not needed at this time.

VIII. Life Insurance

A. Send copies of all premium notices and policy statements to John E. Sestina and Company, for a cost and adequacy review prior to premium payment.

B. _____ should obtain proposals for a $_____-year level term life insurance policy to meet your estate planning goals.

C. Policy:
1. Continue this policy.
2. Continue this policy as it is required under your health insurance plan.
3. Continue this policy as it is provided by your employer at no cost.
4. Continue this policy pending arrival of information for analysis.
5. Consider surrender of this policy.
   a. It is not required to meet your estate planning goals.
6. Surrender of cash value insurance may result in a maximum capital gain of _____.
7. Cash value:
   a. Borrow cash values to pay premiums and interest due at each policy anniversary.
   b. Borrow policy cash value and the cash value of paid-up additions and invest as proposed.
   c. Repay life insurance loan, then reborrow the cash value. Endorse the insurance company check for reinvestment, creating an income tax deduction for investment interest.
   d. Loan interest is deductible investment/nondeductible consumer interest.
8. Premium:
   a. Change premium mode to annual.
   b. The cost is $_____ per thousand and is competitive/uncompetitive with term insurance rates at your current age.
   c. Pay, rather than borrow, future premiums and interest due to ensure the future deductibility of life insurance loan interest. You may periodically borrow future cash value accumulations and invest those sums.
   d. It has a negative cost-per-thousand of _____, which represents positive investment value.

FIGURE D.1 *Continued*

　　　　e. The crossover point for investment versus death benefit is _____ years, and _____ current life expectancy is _____ years.

　　9. Dividends:
　　　　a. Change dividend option to _____.
　　　　b. Withdraw accumulated dividends.

　　10. Owner:
　　　　a. Change ownership from _____ to _____.
　　　　b. Transfer this policy to your proposed irrevocable life insurance trust, or consider replacement if coverage can be obtained at lower cost.

　　11. Beneficiary:
　　　　a. Change primary beneficiary to _____.
　　　　b. Beneficiary designations are as recommended.
　　　　c. Name your _____ contingent or secondary beneficiary.

　　12. Options:
　　　　a. Cancel accidental death provision.

IX.　Health Insurance

　　A. Hospitalization/major medical:
　　　1. Obtain proposals for major medical insurance.
　　　2. Increase deductible to $_____.
　　　3. Major medical coverage is adequate at a competitive cost and requires no supplement.

　　B. Medical expense reimbursement:
　　　1. Consider uninsured medical reimbursement plan.
　　　2. Consider insured medical reimbursement plan.
　　　3. Cancel medical reimbursement plan.

　　C. Long-term care:
　　　1. Consider long-term care insurance.
　　　2. No policy changes are required at this time.

X.　Disability Planning

　　A. Obtain a proposal for $_____ per month of noncancellable disability insurance.

　　B. Discuss corporate reimbursement plan for personally paid disability insurance premiums.

　　C. Obtain a proposal for $_____ per month of group association disability insurance through _____.

FIGURE D.1 *Continued*

D. Obtain proposals for business overhead expense insurance: $____ per month, _____-day wait, and_____-month benefit period.

E. Have corporation reimburse you for disability insurance premiums after _____, 20 _____.

F. Policy:

   1. No policy changes are required at this time.
   2. Cancel this policy, as it is not needed to meet your disability planning goal.
   3. Continue this policy as it is provided by your employer at no/competitive cost to you.
   4. Extend elimination period from present _____ days to _____days.
   5. Extend accident benefit period to life.
   6. Add partial benefit.
   7. Add cost of living increase.
   8. Pay disability premiums corporately.
   9. Pay partial portion of disability premium personally.
   10. Consider canceling business overhead expense insurance.
   11. Compare _____.

XI. Estate Planning

A. Review your estate plan with your attorney.

B. Will:

   1. Amend will(s) for _____ to coordinate with the proposed trusts.
   2. Include a "no contest" clause:
      a. One way to discourage challenge to your will is to include an "anticontest" provision. This provision states that anyone who contests the will automatically forfeits any bequest made to him/her. It does not mean that all contests are legally prohibited. It merely means that challengers will lose their share of your estate if they attempt to interfere with your wishes. Of course, to make this clause work, you must leave potential challengers a meaningful amount—enough so that they will think twice before they rush to their lawyers and start running up legal fees.
   3. Complete a personal property schedule.

C. Trusts:

   1. Execute a revocable self-declaration credit shelter trust for _____.
   2. Living trust:

FIGURE D.1 *Continued*

a. This is a trust you set up during your lifetime that can provide for your living expenses and other benefits while you are alive. Upon your death, it allows for the transfer of whatever property is left to your surviving spouse or other beneficiaries you may name.

b. For the trust to become effective, you must actually fund—or transfer property to—the trust. All too often, people do not change the title on their existing holdings, so the trust has no substance. If property is held in joint names, for example, those assets pass to the joint survivor. If property is held in your name alone, it must go through probate, and will go to the trust only if that is what your will provides.

3. Unified Credit Trust.

4. Consider an irrevocable insurance trust for _____.

5. Establish a statutory grantor retained income trust (GRIT) in order to minimize federal estate tax.

   a. A grantor retained income trust can be set up for a certain term. You get income from the GRIT until it ends; then the principal goes to your beneficiary. Yes, you'll pay a gift tax on the amount you pass on. But it's less than you might fear, because the value of the principal is discounted by the IRS.

6. Consider adding generation-skipping formula to trust to maximize $1,000,000 generation-skipping exemption.

7. Charitable remainder trust.

8. Qualified terminable interest property (QTIP) trust:

   a. Property in which a spouse is given only an interest for his/her life may qualify for the unlimited marital deduction as qualified terminable interest property—or QTIP. If it qualifies, the property will pass to the surviving spouse estate tax free. It will be included in the surviving spouse's estate at death. One of the requirements for qualification as QTIP property is that the executor make an unequivocal election on IRS Form 706, Schedule M, to have it qualify.

9. Qualified personal residence trust (QPRT).

10. Grantor retained annuity trust (GRAT).

D. Sale of principal:

1. Here's an alternative to giving some of your estate away: Sell income-producing property to someone you want to see end up with it anyway. You pay income on any capital gains, but you avoid gift taxes and the higher estate-tax bills that would be levied if you'd held the property while it appreciated. Unlike the GRIT situation, no matter when you die, the property remains outside your estate because you've sold it. Watch

---

FIGURE D.1 *Continued*

out, though: If you undervalue the property at all, it automatically returns to your estate. To be safe, transfer only assets with indisputable values, such as securities and cash, not art or real estate.

E. Split purchase:
1. Instead of buying property that will be part of your estate, buy it with your child. Your payment will purchase a right to the stream of income from the property; your child's payment will buy the right to the property itself after you pass away. Since your heir in effect immediately owns the property at your death, it's not included in your estate. What's more, you can write off your purchase price on a prorated basis over your life expectancy. A danger: Don't give the child the money outright to buy the property, or the IRS may deem the transfer a bequest and your estate will have to pay the taxes on it.

F. Powers of attorney:
1. Execute durable powers of attorney for _____.
    a. This allows someone else to act for you in the event of your disability or incapacity. A regular power of attorney gives someone else the authority to act for you, but that authority automatically ceases if you become incompetent. In such cases, it is necessary to start probate proceedings in order to appoint a personal representative for you. A durable power of attorney avoids the need to go to probate court because it survives your disability or legal incompetence. By naming someone to act as your "attorney in fact," that person is authorized to sign checks, enter contracts, buy or sell real estate, enter safe-deposit boxes, run your business, make transfers to your trust and, in some cases, make health-care decisions on your behalf. Since this gives that person tremendous power, be careful about whom you select.
    b. Amend durable powers of attorney to name successor attorneys-in-fact and add specific power to make gifts.
    c. Execute durable powers of attorney for health care and living wills.

G. Private annuity.

H. Private foundation.

I. Consider second-to-die life insurance.

J. Consider making two $675,000 maximum credit shelter gifts to children.

K   Change ownership of _____ from joint to _____.

L. Gifts:
1. Gift _____ to _____.
2. Gift interest in residence from husband to wife.

FIGURE D.1 *Continued*

3. Gift fractional real estate interest. Instead of giving cash, you could also give a $10,000/$20,000 fractional interest in a piece of real estate (such as a vacation home) each year by deeding over, for example, a one-fifth interest of a $100,000 piece of property annually over a five-year period. However, a new deed would have to be drawn each year. Then, after five years the vacation home is out of your estate.

4. Gift fractional business asset. The same thing could be done with a partnership interest in a personal or business asset.

M. SCINs:

1. These are self-cancellation installment notes. They work this way. Example: You lend $100,000 to your child. The loan is set up with 10 notes of $10,000 each. One is to be repaid each year. However, as each note falls due, you forgive it. Downside: If you die with the notes still in your estate, they are includable for estate tax purposes.

N. Letter of instructions:

1. Your letter of instruction should cover the following items and events:

a. Burial.

O. There may be an Ohio estate tax from the death of the first spouse if your children are beneficiaries of the bypass trust.

P. Review capital requirements in event of _____'s death.

Q. Provide a disclaimer clause.

R. Income in respect of a decedent:

1. Generally, when you inherit assets they are subject to the step up in basis rule; your tax cost is stepped up to the asset's date-of-death value. However, this does not apply to income that was earned by the decedent but was not paid before death. This after-death income may be subject both to income tax in the recipient's hands and to estate tax. There is, however, a deduction on the estate tax return for the income tax paid.

a. Pensions are treated the same as income in respect to a decedent and are subject to double taxation. Lump-sum pension distributions may be subject to an additional 15% excise tax if they exceed the amount of $750,000. A surviving spouse can elect to roll over a pension distribution into an IRA and defer the payment of income tax.

XII. Retirement Planning

A. In order to meet your retirement goals, you must invest $_____ per year, increasing with inflation, in addition to your current _____ contributions.

FIGURE D.1 *Continued*

B. As of 1994, you are no longer able to contribute $30,000 per year to your profit sharing/pension plan. Consider adoption of a complimentary pension/profit sharing plan.

C. IRA (Individual Retirement Account):
   1. Establish an IRA with Charles Schwab & Co. for _____.
   2. Make nondeductible IRA contributions to _____ IRA as soon as possible/in January 20 ____.
   3. Beneficiary designations are as recommended.
   4. Make _____ the primary beneficiary and _____ the contingent beneficiary of _____'s IRA.

D. SEP (Simplified Employee Pension) Plan:
   1. Establish a SEP plan by adopting the Charles Schwab & Co. prototype.
   2. Maximize contributions to SEP plan this year.
   3. Make _____ SEP plan contributions as soon as possible.
   4. Terminate SEP plan.
   5. Beneficiary designations are as recommended.
   6. Make _____ the primary beneficiary and _____ the contingent beneficiary of _____'s SEP.

E. 403(b) (Tax-Sheltered Annuity) Plan:
   1. Establish a 403(b) tax-sheltered annuity plan through _____.
   2. Have plan administrator calculate your maximum allowable contribution, using the three alternative calculation methods.
   3. Maximize contributions to 403(b) plan this year.
   4. Beneficiary designations are as recommended.
   5. Make _____ the primary beneficiary and _____ the contingent beneficiary of _____'s 403(b) plan.
   6. Change investment allocations as recommended.

F. 401(k) Plan:
   1. Maximize contributions to 401(k) plan this year.
   2. Change 401(k) plan investment allocations as recommended.

G. Profit-Sharing Plan:
   1. Maximize contributions to profit-sharing plan this year.
   2. Amend/establish profit-sharing plan to provide for employee loans/voluntary contributions/integration with Social Security/disability benefits.
   3. Your plan will need to be amended to comply with the Tax Reform Act (TRA) of 1986. Please send copy of amended/restated plan.

FIGURE D.1 *Continued*

4. Consider the following changes when amending your plan:
   a. Change vesting schedule to _____.
   b. Eliminate participant loan provisions.
   c. Change Social Security integration levels to $____ and _____%.
5. Request that plan administrator accurately determine after-tax contribution basis for voluntary account.
6. Recalculate I.R.C. Sec. 415 limit for _____.
7. The maximum allowable contribution for _____ to the profit-sharing plan must be reduced by the amount contributed to his/her 403(b) plan.
8. Beneficiary designations are as recommended.
9. Make _____ the primary beneficiary and _____ the contingent beneficiary of _____'s profit-sharing plan.

H. Money Purchase Pension Plan:
1. Maximize contributions to pension plan this year.
2. Amend/establish pension plan to provide for employee loans/voluntary contributions/integration with Social Security/disability benefits.
3. Your plan will need to be amended to comply with the Tax Reform Act (TRA) of 1986. Please send copy of amended/restated plan.
4. Consider the following changes when amending your plan:
   a. Change vesting schedule to six-year graded/three-year cliff.
   b. Eliminate participant loan provisions.
   c. Change Social Security integration levels to $____ and ____%.
5. Request that plan administrator accurately determine after-tax contribution basis for voluntary account.
6. Recalculate I.R.C. Sec. 415 limit for _____.
7. The maximum allowable contribution for _____ to the pension plan must be reduced by the amount contributed to his/her 403(b) plan.
8. Beneficiary designations are as recommended.
9. Make _____ the primary beneficiary and _____ the contingent beneficiary of _____'s pension plan.

I. Defined Benefit Pension Plan
1. The Omnibus Budget Reconciliation Act (OBRA) of 1987 requires that, for plan years beginning after 1988, quarterly contributions must be made to a defined benefit pension plan.
2. Recalculate I.R.C. Sec. 415 limit for _____.
3. Maximize contributions to defined benefit plan this year.
4. Your plan will need to be amended to comply with the Tax Reform Act (TRA) of 1986. Please send copy of amended plan.

FIGURE D.1 *Continued*

5. The maximum allowable contribution for _____ to the defined benefit pension plan must be reduced by the amount contributed to his/her 403(b) plan.

6. Beneficiary designations are as recommended.

7. Make _____ the primary beneficiary and _____ the contingent beneficiary of _____'s pension plan.

8. Review qualified plan administration guidelines.

J. Deferred Compensation Plan/Supplemental Executive Retirement Plan (SERP)—Nonqualified

1. Establish a Deferred Compensation Plan /Supplemental Executive Retirement Plan (SERP) with _____.

2. Contribute _____ to deferred compensation plan this year.

3. Beneficiary designations are as recommended.

4. Make _____ the primary beneficiary and _____ the contingent beneficiary of the deferred compensation plan/SERP.

K. The beneficiaries of all _____'s nonqualified retirement plans should be:

1. Primary:

2. Contingent:

XIII. Dependent Planning

A. Apply for Social Security numbers(s) for _____.

B. Establish Sec. 2503 (c) trust for _____.

C. Establish a Crummey trust:

1. Unlike the Section 2503(c) trust and the UGMA rules, the trust assets do not have to flow to the beneficiary child by age 21. The beneficiary can exercise the right to withdraw a specified amount from the trust each year; however, the trust assets are kept intact. This can be achieved only to a limited extent, under Section 2503(c), when there are multiple beneficiaries.

2. Clients using Crummey or Section 2503(c) trusts as vehicles for funding college education must be on guard; when income from trust funds is used to pay education expenses that are considered to be the obligation of the grantor, the trust income may be taxed to the grantor.

D. Establish custodial account at Charles Schwab & Co. under Ohio Transfers to Minors Act for _____, with as _____ custodian.

E. Make an interest-free loan to _____ for $10,000.

FIGURE D.1 *Continued*

F. Gift appreciated investment property to child. This will minimize the tax on the eventual capital gain.

G. Employ child in business.

H. Have child apply for college aid/student loan.

I. Borrow from your 401(k) plan:
   1. Typically, loans made out of qualified employee retirement plans are generally treated as distributions, and therefore are taxable to the recipient of the proceeds. However, exceptions do exist with regard to 401(k) plans. Certain loan proceeds used to pay higher education expenses are exempted from the general rules of taxability. These loans must be for less than $50,000 and repaid within five years. If one-half of the present value of the nonforfeitable benefits of the retirement plan is less than $50,000, then only that amount of the loan qualifies, with a minimum qualified loan of $10,000.

J. Change following investments:

K. Gift-leaseback:
   1. This can be a very favorable planning strategy for the owner of a family business. How it works: A parent who owns a building (or other substantial asset) used in the business establishes a trust for the benefit of a child, donates the building to the trust, then pays rent to the trust for the use of the gifted asset in the family business. The parent gets to deduct the rent as a business expense, while the child receives the rental income at a lower tax rate, thus reducing the family income-tax bill. The building is also removed from the parent's estate.

L. Gift sufficient assets to each child to produce $1,300 of annual investment income.

FIGURE D.1 *Continued*

Third Set of Forms Needed

LETTER OF AUTHORIZATION

Advisor Name
Address

Dear

We hereby authorize you to provide John E. Sestina and Company with information they may request regarding our financial affairs. We have engaged John E. Sestina and Company to analyze our financial data, and to maintain and update this information for our use and the use of our financial advisors.

This letter shall be effective upon receipt and shall remain in effect until further notice. When you send the information that John E. Sestina and Company requests, please send us a copy of your letter listing the information you have provided.

If you have any questions regarding this authorization, please contact us.

Signature

Signature

FIGURE E.1 Letter of Authorization

John E. Sestina and Company

Date

Advisor Name
Address

Dear

Your client, _____, has engaged the financial planning and investment counseling services of John E. Sestina and Company. We would like to take this opportunity to introduce our firm. We are independent, fee-only financial planners. We do not sell any financial products, so we believe that our recommendations are influenced only by our client's circumstances and objectives.

Constant flow of information is critical to the successful development and execution of the client's financial plan. We will assist in accomplishing this through frequent and periodic review and implementation meetings.

We encourage our client's other professional advisors to continue to be or to become actively involved in the financial planning process. We believe that coordination of advisors provides the stimulus that will allow each of us to perform even more effectively for our clients.

Each of our clients is assigned a staff analyst to examine and summarize information and to prepare regular financial updates. Your reception to their call or correspondence would be appreciated.

We have enclosed a copy of the information release authorization signed by _____ for your file as well as our brochure. If you have any questions, please feel free to call.

Sincerely,

John E. Sestina

FIGURE E.2 Letter to Participating Advisors

Guidelines for Selecting a Financial Planner

The key to good financial advice is the competence, ethics, and motivation of the advisor. Ask yourself and others these questions:

1. What is the planner's background and experience in financial advising?

2. What is the advisor's reputation in the community?

3. Does the financial planner work with other reputable professionals such as attorneys, accountants, bankers, and investment advisors to formulate and implement the suggested plan?

4. Can the planner help you to evaluate your current advisors or introduce you to other advisors if you need them?

5. How does the advisor make his or her living? In other words, does the planner get his or her personal compensation from fees only, commissions only, or a combination of the two?

6. Does the planner implement the portion of the plan that compensates him or her (i.e., insurance, investments, tax shelters) before bringing in those who might have alternate recommendations (i.e., attorney, accountant, banker)?

7. Before giving you advice, does the advisor really try to discover your philosophy, priorities, and objectives?

8. Is your marital partner involved and informed at each stage of the planning process?

9. Does the planner first address your high-priority objectives or the objectives that involve commission products?

10. Do both partners feel comfortable with the planner?

11. Does the planner actually follow through and follow up to see that the recommendations you accept are put into action?

12. Does the advisor represent a single product source or company or draw from a number of sources for low cost and high quality in each individual's case?

13. Does the planner accept the approach that produces the most compensation for him or her despite lower-cost alternatives for you (e.g., permanent life insurance versus term)?

FIGURE E.3 Guidelines for Selecting a Financial Planner

14. Does the advisor say that the added cost of his or her product is worth it because of the value of the planner's advice?

15. Does the planner charge a fee for analysis and then sell commission products as "a service"?

16. Does the advisor say that someone will get the commissions, so why not him or her?

17. Are all compensation arrangements clearly disclosed in advance?

18. Are you shown the exact dollar amount the advisor will receive under each alternate recommendation?

19. Does the planner develop a comprehensive plan that addresses cash flow, education, retirement, employee benefits, taxes, investments, risk management, business planning, estate planning, and other specific needs you might have?

20. Does the planner have any fiduciary responsibility?

21. Are you given a copy of the planner's ADV form?

You must evaluate the answers to these questions before selecting a financial planner. Taking of commissions is not automatically bad. Many top-notch planners are commission-only. You should be fully aware of this, however, to properly interpret the advice and the cost of the advice you receive.

FIGURE E.3 *Continued*

OMB APPROVAL

OMB No.: 3235-0049
Expires: June 30, 1991
Estimated average burden
hours per response 8.96

FORM ADV
Part II - Page 1   **Uniform Application for Investment Advisor Registration**

Name of Investment Advisor:
SESTINA, BUDROS & RUHLIN, INC.

Address:	(Number and Street)	(City)	State)	(Zip Code)	Area Code:	Telephone Number:
	3726-J Olentangy River Rd.	Columbus	OH	43214	(614	457-8200

This part of Form ADV gives information about the investment advisor and its business for the use of clients.
The information has not been approved or verified by any government authority.

Table of Contents

(Schedules A, B, C, D, and E are included with Part I of this Form, for the use of regulatory bodies, and are not distributed to clients.)

FIGURE E.4 Uniform Application for Investment Advisor Registration (ADV)

Applicant:	SEC File Number:	Date:
SESTINA, BUDROS & RUHLIN, INC.	801- 32884	7-27-88

Definitions for Part II

Related person—Any officer, director or partner of applicant or any person directly or indirectly controlling, controlled by, or under common control with the applicant, including any non-clerical, non-ministerial employer.

Investment Supervisory Services—Giving continuous investment advice to a client (or making investments for the client) based on the individual needs of the client. Individual needs include, for example, the nature of other client assets and the client's personal and family obligations.

---

1. **A. Advisory Services and Fees.** (check the applicable boxes)

   Applicant:

   For each type of service provided, state the approximate % of total advisory billings from that service. (See instruction below.)

   ☒ (1) Provides investment supervisory services .... _15_ %
   ☒ (2) Manages investment advisory accounts not involving investment supervisory services .... _15_ %
   ☐ (3) Furnishes investment advice through consultations not included in either service described above .... _____ %
   ☐ (4) Issues periodicals about securities by subscription .... _____ %
   ☐ (5) Issues special reports about securities not included in any service described above .... _____ %
   ☐ (6) Issues, not as part of any service described above, any charts, graphs, formulas, or other devices which clients may use to evaluate securities .... _____ %
   ☒ (7) On more than an occasional basis, furnishes advice to clients on matters not involving securities .... _70_ %
   ☐ (8) Provides a timing service... _____ %
   ☐ (9) Furnishes advice about securities in any manner not described above .... _____ %

   (Percentages should be based on applicant's last fiscal year. If applicant has not completed its first fiscal year, provide estimates of advisory billings for that year and state that the percentages are estimates.)

   B. Does applicant call any of the services it checked above financial planning or some similar term? ....   Yes ☒   No ☐

   C. Applicant offers investment advisory services for: (check all that apply)

   ☒ (1) A percentage of assets under management   ☐ (4) Subscription fees
   ☐ (2) Hourly charges   ☐ (5) Commissions
   ☐ (3) Fixed fees (not including subscription fees)   ☐ (6) Other

   D. For each checked box in A above, describe on Schedule F:

   • the services provided, including the name of any publication or report issued by the advisor on a subscription basis or for a fee

   • applicant's basic fee schedule, how fees are charged and whether its fees are negotiable

   • when compensation is payable, and if compensation is payable before service is provided, how a client may get a refund or may terminate an investment advisory contract before its expiration date

2. **Types of Clients** — Applicant generally provides investment advice to: (check those that apply)

   ☒ A. Individuals   ☒ E. Trusts, estates, or charitable organizations

   ☐ B. Banks or thrift institutions   ☒ F. Corporations or business entities other than those listed above

   ☐ C. Investment companies
                                                  ☐ G. Other (describe on Schedule F)
   ☒ D. Pension and profit sharing plans

Answer all Items. Complete amended pages in full, circle amended items and file with execution page (page 1).

FIGURE E.4 *Continued*

Applicant:	SEC File Number:	Date:
SESTINA, BUDROS & RUHLIN, INC.	801- 32884	7-27-88

3. Types of Investments. Applicant offers advice on the following: (check those that apply)

	A.	Equity Securities	☒ H.	Unites States government securities
☒		(1) exchange-listed securities		
☒		(2) securities traded over-the-counter		I. Options contracts on:
☒		(3) foreign issuers	☒	(1) securities
			☒	(2) commodities
☒	B.	Warrants		
				J. Futures contracts on:
☒	C.	Corporate debt securities	☐	(1) tangibles
		(other than commercial paper)	☐	(2) intangibles
☒	D.	Commercial paper		K. Interests in partnerships investing in:
			☒	(1) real estate
☒	E.	Certificates of deposit	☒	(2) oil and gas interests
			☒	(3) other (explain on Schedule F)
☒	F.	Municipal securities		
			☐	L. Other (explain on Schedule F)
	G.	Investment company securities:		
☒		(1) variable life insurance		
☒		(2) variable annuities		
☒		(3) mutual fund shares		

4. Methods of Analysis, Sources of Information, and Investment Strategies.

A. Applicant's security analysis methods include: (check those that apply)

(1) ☐ Charting   (4) ☐ Cyclical

(2) ☒ Fundamental   (5) ☐ Other (explain on Schedule F)

(3) ☒ Technical

B. The main sources of information applicant uses include: (check those that apply)

(1) ☒ Financial newspapers and magazines   (5) ☒ Timing services

(2) ☐ Inspections of corporate activities   (6) ☒ Annual reports, prospectuses, filings with the Securities and Exchange Commission

(3) ☒ Research materials prepared by others   (7) ☒ Company press releases

(4) ☒ Corporate rating services   (8) ☐ Other (explain on Schedule F)

C. The investment strategies used to implement any investment advice given to clients include: (check those that apply)

(1) ☒ Long term purchases (securities held at least a year)   (5) ☒ Margin transactions

(2) ☒ Short term purchases (securities sold within a year)   (6) ☒ Option writing, including covered options, uncovered options or spreading strategies

(3) ☒ Trading (securities sold within 30 days)   (7) ☐ Other (explain on Schedule F)

(4) ☒ Short sales

Answer all Items. Complete amended pages in full, circle amended items and file with execution page (page 1).

FIGURE E.4 *Continued*

Applicant:	SEC File Number:	Date:
SESTINA, BUDROS & RUHLIN, INC.	801- 32884	JAN. 7, 1991

5. **Education and Business Standards.**

Are there any general standards of education or business experience that applicant requires of those involved in determining or giving investment advice to clients? .... Yes ☒ No ☐

(If yes, describe these standards on Schedule F.)

6. **Education and Business Background.**

For:

- each member of the investment committee or group that determines general investment advice to be given to clients, or
- if the applicant has no investment committee or group, each individual who determines general investment advice given to clients (if more than five, respond only for their supervisors)
- each principal executive officer of applicant or each person with similar status or performing similar functions.

On Schedule F, give the:

- name
- year of birth
- formal education after high school
- business background for the preceding five years

7. **Other Business Activities.** (check those that apply)

☐ A. Applicant is actively engaged in a business other than giving investment advice.

☐ B. Applicant sells products or services other than investment advice to clients.

☒ C. The principal business of applicant or its principal executive officers involves something other than providing investment advice.

(For each checked box describe the other activities, including the time spent on them, on Schedule F.)

8. **Other Financial Industry Activities or Affiliations.** (check those that apply)

☐ A. Applicant is registered (or has an application pending) as a securities broker-dealer.

☐ B. Applicant is registered (or has an application pending) as a futures commission merchant, commodity pool operator or commodity trading advisor.

C. Applicant has arrangements that are material to its advisory business or its clients with a related person who is a:

☐	(1) broker-dealer	☐	(7) accounting firm
☐	(2) investment company	☐	(8) law firm
☐	(3) other investment advisor	☐	(9) insurance company or agency
☐	(4) financial planning firm	☐	(10) pension consultant
☐	(5) commodity pool operator, commodity trading adviser or futures commission merchant	☐	(11) real estate broker or dealer
		☐	(12) entity that creates or packages limited partnerships
☐	(6) banking or thrift institution		

(For each checked box in C, on Schedule F identify the related person and describe the relationship and the arrangements.)

D. Is applicant or a related person a general partner in any partnership in which clients are solicited to invest? .... Yes ☐ No ☒

(If yes, describe on Schedule F the partnerships and what they invest in.)

Answer all Items. Complete amended pages in full, circle amended items and file with execution page (page 1).

FIGURE E.4 *Continued*

Applicant:	SEC File Number:	Date:
SESTINA, BUDROS & RUHLIN, INC.	801- 32884	Jan. 7, 1991

---

9. **Participation or Interest in Client Transactions.**

   Applicant or a related person: (check those that apply)

   ☐ A.   As principal, buys securities for itself from or sells securities it owns to any client.

   ☐ B.   As broker or agent effects securities transactions for compensation for any client.

   ☐ C.   As broker or agent for any person other than a client effects transactions in which client securities are sold to or bought from a brokerage customer.

   ☐ D.   Recommends to clients that they buy or sell securities or investment products in which the applicant or a related person has some financial interest.

   ☐ E.   Buys or sells for itself securities that it also recommends to clients.

   (For each box checked, describe on Schedule F when the applicant or a related person engages in these transactions and what restrictions, internal procedures, or disclosures are used for conflicts of interest in those transactions.)

---

10. **Conditions for Managing Accounts.** Does the applicant provide investment supervisory services, manage investment advisory accounts or hold itself out as providing financial planning or some similarly termed services *and* impose a minimum dollar value of assets or other conditions for starting or maintaining an account?......................................   Yes ☐   No ☒

   (If yes, describe on Schedule F.)

---

11. **Review of Accounts.** If applicant provides investment supervisory services, manages investment advisory accounts, or holds itself out as providing financial planning or some similarly termed services:

   A.   Describe below the reviews and reviewers of the accounts. **For reviews**, include their frequency, different levels, and triggering factors. **For reviewers**, include the number of reviewers, their titles and functions, instructions they receive from applicant on performing reviews, and number of accounts assigned each.

   FOR REVIEWS: Advisor reviews all accounts no less than quarterly with an annual review. At each review, a portfolio valuation statement is prepared along with current recommendations and correspondence concerning implementation of financial planning and investment matters.

   FOR REVIEWERS: The advisor employs three (3) financial planners who review each account no less than quarterly. Financial planners have varying functions. Each account is also reviewed by an analyst for the preparation of the investment and financial planning data and implementation instructions. The advisor initiates the reviews and is a matter of company policy. Each analyst has approximately 30 accounts assigned. The financial planners do not have assigned accounts, but individually or collectively review each.

   B.   Describe below the nature and frequency of regular reports to clients on their accounts.

   A full financial planning report of annual review for clients is prepared once a year. In addition, a quarterly investment portfolio analysis and valuation is prepared which accompanies a financial planning status and implementation report.

Answer all Items. Complete amended pages in full, circle amended items and file with execution page (page 1).

FIGURE E.4 *Continued*

Applicant:	SEC File Number:	Date:
SESTINA, BUDROS & RUHLIN, INC.	801- 32884	Jan. 7, 1991

12. Investment or Brokerage Discretion.

A. Does applicant or any related person have authority to determine, without obtaining specific client consent, the:

(1) securities to be bought or sold? .... Yes ☐ No ☒

(2) amount of the securities to be bought or sold? .... Yes ☐ No ☒

(3) broker or dealer to be used? .... Yes ☐ No ☒

(4) commission rates paid? .... Yes ☐ No ☒

B. Does applicant or a related person suggest brokers to clients? .... Yes ☒ No ☐

For each yes answer to A describe on Schedule F any limitations on the authority. For each yes to A(3), A(4) or B, describe on Schedule F the factors considered in selecting brokers and determining the reasonableness of their commissions. If the value of products, research and services given to the applicant or a related person is a factor, describe:

- the products, research and services

- whether clients may pay commissions higher than those obtainable from other brokers in return for those products and services

- whether research is used to service all of applicant's accounts or just those accounts paying for it; and

- any procedures the applicant used during the last fiscal year to direct client transactions to a particular broker in return for products and research services received.

13. Additional Compensation.

Does the applicant or a related person have any arrangements, oral or in writing, where it:

A. is paid cash by or receives some economic benefit (including commissions, equipment or non-research services) from a non-client in connection with giving advice to clients? .... Yes ☐ No ☒

B. directly or indirectly compensates any person for client referrals? .... Yes ☐ No ☒

(For each yes, describe the arrangements on Schedule F.)

14. Balance Sheet. Applicant must provide a balance sheet for the most recent fiscal year on Schedule G if applicant:

- has custody of client funds or securities; or

- requires prepayment of more than $500 in fees per client and 6 or more months in advance

Has applicant provided a Schedule G balance sheet? .... Yes ☐ No ☒

Answer all Items. Complete amended pages in full, circle amended items and file with execution page (page 1).

FIGURE E.4 *Continued*

(Do not use this Schedule as a continuation sheet for Form ADV Part I or any other schedules.)

I. Full name of applicant exactly as stated in Item IA of Part I of Form ADV: SESTINA, BUDROS & RUHLIN, INC.	IRS Empl. Ident. No.: 31-1237051

Item of Form (identify)	Answer
Part II 1.D.	Advisor provides investment advisory services and furnishes advice to clients on matters not involving securities only as a part of a total financial planning process. The minimum fee includes fees for full service financial planning and investment management services. In certain instances, depending upon the client's needs and the services to be performed by Advisor, a contract may be entered into with a fee different from the fee schedule set forth below. This fee would be based upon individual negotiations with the particular client within the range of fees set forth below under Minimum and Maximum Fees. A client can terminate at anytime. The refund will not exceed one-half the annual fee. After six months the refund is pro rata by month. The following fees are charged on an annual basis and may be prepaid, at the election of the client, or paid as services are provided. However, the total investment management fee may not be required to be prepaid more than six months in advance.

PERSONAL FINANCIAL ADVISORY FEE

Business Owner/Self Employed		Non-Business Owner	
4% of Earned Income	1st Year	2% of Earned Income	1st Year
3% of Earned Income	2nd Year	1% of Earned Income	2nd Year
2% of Earned Income	3rd Year	1% of Earned Income	3rd Year
1% of Earned Income	4th Year	1% of Earned Income	4th Year

INVESTMENT MANAGEMENT FEE

$1.00 to $500,000 of Investment Assets	1%
$500,001 to $1,000,000 of Investment Assets	3/4 of 1%
$1,000,001 or more of Investment Assets	1/2 of 1%

MINIMUM AND MAXIMUM FEES

Minimum fee - 1st year...................$ 3,500
Minimum fee - 2nd year and thereafter....$ 2,500
Maximum fee............................$50,000

FIFTH YEAR AND THEREAFTER

For fifth year clients and thereafter, the fee is the Investment Management Fee only.

Complete amended pages in full, circle amended items and file with execution page (page 1).

FIGURE E.4 *Continued*

Applicant: SESTINA, BUDROS & RUHLIN, INC.	SEC File Number: 801- 32884	Date: Jan. 7, 1991

(Do not use this Schedule as a continuation sheet for Form ADV Part I or any other schedules.)

I. Full name of applicant exactly as stated in Item 1A. of Part I of Form ADV: SESTINA, BUDROS & RUHLIN, INC.	IRS Empl. Ident. No.: 31-1237051

Item of Form (identify)	Answer
Part II 3.K.	Advisor may offer advice on partnership investing in business interests other than real estate or oil and gas.
Part II 5.	College graduate and former vocational business and/or investment experience.
Part II 7.C.	Advisor provides investment advisory services and furnishes advice to clients on matters not involving securities only as a part of a total financial planning process.
Part II 12.B.	Advisor may recommend a broker to a client who does not have an active relationship with a broker. The advisor considers past performance, personal relationship and associations with a national or regional brokerage firm in recommending a broker, but the advisor does not determine the reasonableness of the broker's commission, as the engagement of any recommended broker is at the exclusive discretion of the client.

Complete amended pages in full, circle amended items and file with execution page (page 1).

FIGURE E.4 *Continued*

Financial Planning Book Table of Contents

1. **Memo's/Notes**
   a. Questionnaire
   b. Documentation Checklist
   c. Complete Implementation Checklist for Recommendations

2. **Important Information**
   a. Important Information Summary
   b. Advisor Information Summary
   c. Safe-Deposit Box/Marriage-Separation/Inheritance Summary
   d. Goal Summary

3. **Income Analysis**
   a. Cash Flow Forecast Current Lifestyle
   b. Income Tax Projection

4. **Balance Sheets**
   a. Consolidated, Husband, Wife, Joint, Dependent
   b. Comparative

5. **Assets**
   a. Checking/Savings Accounts
   b. Residence
   c. Auto
   d. Personal Property Inventory

6. **Liabilities—Home/Car/Credit Cards Summary**
   a. Liability Summary
   b. Credit Cards Summary
   c. Credit Bureau Copy

7. **Investments**
   a. Portfolio Model
   b. Record Percentage in Growth/Nongrowth
   c. Investment Accounts Summary
   d. 401(k) Summary
   e. Morningstar Average Matrix

8. **Business Interests**
   a. Business Interests Summary

9. **Life Insurance**
   a. Life Insurance Summary—Husband
   b. Life Insurance Summary—Wife

FIGURE E.5 Financial Planning Book Table of Contents

10. **Health Insurance**
    a. Health Insurance Summary
    b. Dental/Vision Summary
    c. Long-Term Care Summary
    d. Medigap Summary

11. **Property Casualty Insurance**
    a. Home Insurance Summary
    b. Auto Insurance Summary
    c. Umbrella Insurance Summary

12. **Retirement Planning**
    a. Retirement Planning Assumptions to Reach Goal
    b Defined Benefit Plan Summary
    c. Social Security Benefits Statement

13. **Dependent Planning**
    a. Education Funding Summary

14. **Disability Planning**
    a. Disability Insurance Summary

15. **Estate Planning**
    a. Estate Planning Summary
    b. Letter of Instructions Worksheet
    c. Record Keeping Worksheet: Attach to Letter of Instructions
    d. Safe-Deposit Box Inventory: Attach to Letter of Instructions
    e. Man's Will Summary
    f. Woman's Will Summary
    g. Man's Revocable Trust Summary
    h. Woman's Revocable Trust Summary
    i. Man's Irrevocable Trust Summary
    j. Woman's Irrevocable Trust Summary
    k. Charitable Trust Summary
    l. Man's Durable Power of Attorney Summary
    m. Woman's Durable Power of Attorney Summary
    n. Man's Health Care Proxy Summary
    o. Woman's Health Care Proxy Summary
    p. Man's Living Will Summary
    q. Woman's Living Will Summary

FIGURE E.5 *Continued*

FIRST PRESENTATION CHECKLIST

In general, make the name of an item (e.g., Investment) as complete as possible—TRP Equity Income as opposed to TRP Eq Inc. Make certain the names are consistent—not Bank One Ckg on one and then National City Chk on the next one.

Names of accounts should also be consistent (i.e., Schwab-H, Schwab-W, Schwab-J, Schwab-IRA-H, Schwab-IRAro-H, Schwab-PEN-H, Schwab-PS-H, Home Mortgage-J, Home Equity Loan-W, etc.).

Review each section for missing data or blanks in the client spreadsheet. If something is unknown, blank, or missing, request it in advance of the meeting.

1. Set up Client data file box.
   a. Sort and file client data into file box with manila files.
3. Set up three-ring binder.
   a. Prepare tabs.
   b. Complete all summary forms in the Client Master Book.
4. Set up Quicken, including financial planner information.
5. Set up "Planner Notes.doc" for your comments and recommendations. Do not make your changes in the "Client Meeting Notes."
6. Set up "Client Meeting Notes."
   a. Set up table for name, date of birth, social security number, and so on.

Man	Birth	SS#
Woman	Birth	SS#
Anniversary	Date	
Child 1,2,3, etc.	Birth	SS#
Allocation	90%	10%
Refreshment	Coffee, etc.	Tea with cream
Coplanner		

7. Review "Documentation Checklist" and send copy to the client requesting the missing data be brought to the next meeting or sent in advance.
8. Complete "Implementation Checklist."
9. Put Table of Contents in client's book.
10. Send to client to bring completed to first meeting.
    a. "Letter of Confirmation."
    b. "Cash Flow Forecast."

FIGURE E.6 First Presentation Checklist/Annual Planning Checklist

11. Calculate life insurance cost per thousand for each policy.

12. Prepare letters:
    a. Duplicate authorization of statements.
    b. Updated life insurance policy information.

13. Scan:
    a. Corporate tax return and balance sheet or schedule C.
    b. Personal federal and state tax returns in their entirety.
    c. All estate planning documents, including wills, trusts, and so on.

ANNUAL PLANNING CHECKLIST

In addition to rechecking the above:

1. Review old memos.

2. Redo client data box labels and check data files.

3. Clean out client book.

4. Leave two years' cash flow in our book, original worksheet in client book.

5. Prepare letters for updated life insurance policy information.

FIGURE E.6 *Continued*

Update Checklist

In general, make the name of an item (e.g., Investment) as complete as possible—TRP Equity Income as opposed to TRP Eq Inc. There is no need to add the word "Fund" to the title. Make certain the names are consistent—not Bank One Ckg on one and then National City Chk on the next one.

Names of accounts should also be consistent. For example:

Schwab-H	Husband
Schwab-W	Wife
Schwab-J	Jointly owned
Schwab-IRA-DD-H	Deductible IRA
Schwab-IRA-ND-W	Nondeductible IRA
Schwab-IRAro-H	Rollover IRA
Schwab-IRA-Roth-W	Roth IRA
Schwab-PEN-DB-H	Defined Benefit Pension
Schwab-PEN-MP-W	Money Purchase Pension
Schwab-PS-H	Profit Sharing
Home Mortgage-J	Home Mortgage
Home Equity Loan-H	Home Equity Loan

Review each section for missing data or blanks in the client spreadsheet. If something is unknown, blank, or missing, request it from the client in advance of the meeting.

Keep a scanned copy of every application for a broker, insurance company, etc.

1. **Notes**
   a. Read memos.
   b. Check Implementation Checklist. Mark off whatever has been done. These completed items should be posted in your "Planner Notes" and transferred to the "Client Meeting Notes" after discussion with other planner prior to the client meeting.
   c. Check for memos with recommendations, which should be on the checklist and add to implementation checklist/To-do items where necessary.
   d. Make notes on memos to clarify or update information.
   e. Route letters from client's advisors, then scan and put in the Notes section. All Sestina letters should be in the client Word Meeting Notes file. This does not apply to simple "enclosure" letters.
   f. Check for scanned current Sestina authorization letters.
   g. Check for scanned duplicate statements to Sestina.
   h. Review "Financial Planning Checklist" to see when the "Review Date" is for the item.

2. **Important Information**
   a. Add any improvements to residence real estate page and add to the cost basis.

FIGURE E.7 Update Checklist

3. *Income Analysis*
   a. Review current personal tax returns (federal and state).
   b. Scan tax returns to this client folder.

4. *Balance Sheet*
   a. Confirm balances in Quicken are correct for each of the Husband, Wife, and Joint reports.
   b. Prepare Excel Balance Sheet.
      i. Print Quicken Balance Sheet to Client.prn file and then import to spreadsheet.
   c. Create a balance sheet report in Quicken to reflect the loan against the property to which it pertains.

5. *Assets*

6. *Liabilities*
   a. Check second mortgages to be sure they are under Home Mortgage in chart of accounts. Make sure qualifier of loan matches qualifier of residence.
   b. Add personal, open-end car leases (leased car value and current payoff amount) to balance sheet. Remove closed-end and company-leased cars.
   c. Note on liability page when mortgage insurance covers the outstanding principal balance.

7. *Investments*
   a. Confirm investment name in Quicken agrees with the Morningstar name.
   b. Change name of account if brokerage name changes.
   c. Update Buy/Sell spreadsheet.
      i. In Quicken, create memorized "Portfolio by Account" Report if it does not exist.
         1. Subtotal by Account.
         2. Do not show cents.
      ii. Print the report to a Client.prn file in the Client folder.
      iii. Import the file to Excel (the delimiter is comma).
      iv. Eliminate all columns except "Security" and "Balance."
      v. Copy to the "Buy/Sell" worksheet in client book.
      vi. Make certain the commas appear in the numbers of both columns.
      vii. Eliminate pennies.
      vii. Set up "Freeze Panes."
      ix. Bold names of accounts.
   d. Update Client Morningstar.
      i. In Quicken using the Portfolio View:
         1. Select "Group By."
         2. Choose "Security."
         3. Print security listing so you have security name and dollar amounts.
         4. Input dollar amounts of each security into Morningstar.

FIGURE E.7 *Continued*

    e. Add surrender charges to annuities permanent page.

    f. If an account has been rolled over to, say, Schwab, then rename the account and preserve the basis information. The alternative is to export the information from the old account and import it into the new Schwab account.

8. **Business Interests**
   a. Review corporate tax returns and then scan in Business Interest section on computer.
   b. Review all agreements for comments or recommendations.

9. **Life Insurance**
   a. Check all beneficiary designations. If not listed, put either "unknown" or "none designated."
   b. Add interest rate to life insurance page if dividends are accumulating.

10. **Property and Casualty Insurance**
    a. Add homeowners and auto insurance renewal dates to Implementation Checklist.
    b. Add "Workers' Compensation" and certificate number to Property/Casualty Summary page.
    c. Scan premium notice statements.

11. **Health Insurance**

12. **Retirement Planning**
    a. For retirement plans that we track, update employee liability.
    b. Add contributions to permanent page each time a contribution is made for all retirement plans. Indicate the year for which the contribution was made in the memo section of the Quicken transaction as follows: 1999 contribution.
    c. Check all beneficiary designations. If not listed, put either "unknown" or "none designated."

13. **Dependent Planning**
    a. Add a page to track gifts to children.

14. **Disability Planning**

15. **Estate Planning**
    a. Scan all documents to the Estate Planning folder of the client.

FIGURE E.7 *Continued*

**AUTHORIZATION FOR
DUPLICATE CONFIRMATION STATEMENTS**

Name of Investment
Name on Account
Account Number

To whom it may concern:

This letter is your authorization to send duplicate statements and confirmations with regard to my/our above-referenced account to the following:

John E. Sestina and Company
6460 Fiesta Drive
Columbus, OH 43235

This authorization should also apply for any accounts set up with the same registration.

This authorization will remain in effect until you receive a revocation in writing.

Sincerely,

Signature   Date

Signature   Date

FIGURE E.8 Authorization for Duplicate Confirmation Statements

APPENDIX F

Client Master

Financial Planning Checklist

Start Date: 9/7/00
Client Name: Name

*Give at Start of Relationship   **Book Information**

*	Date Given	Date Received	Date Completed	Review Date	
					1 Memo's/Notes
1				12/30/00	Questionnaire
1				12/30/00	Documentation Checklist
				12/30/00	Complete Implementation Checklist for Recommendations
					2 Important Information
				12/30/00	Important Information Summary
				12/30/00	Advisor Information Summary
				12/30/00	Safe-Deposit Box / Marriage-Separation/ Inheritance Summary
1				12/30/00	Goal Summary
					3 Income Analysis
1				12/30/00	Cash Flow Forecast Current Lifestyle
				12/30/00	9 Adjust for Life Insurance Needs
				12/30/00	14 Adjust for Disability Insurance Needs
				12/30/00	3 Complete QFP Cash flow
				12/30/00	12 Retirement Needs
				12/30/00	9 Life Insurance Needs - Man
				12/30/00	9 Life Insurance Needs - Woman
				12/30/00	13 Education Plan
				12/30/00	14 Disability Insurance Needs - Man
				12/30/00	14 Disability Insurance Needs - Woman
				12/30/00	Income Tax Projection
					4 Balance Sheets
				12/30/00	Consolidated, Husband, Wife, Joint, Dependent
				12/30/00	Comparative
					5 Assets
				12/30/00	Checking/Savings Accounts
				12/30/00	Residence
				12/30/00	Auto
				12/30/00	Personal Property Inventory
2				12/30/00	Household Inventory, Blank Pages for Inventory
					6 Liabilities – Home/Car/Credit Cards Summary
				12/30/00	Liability Summary
				12/30/00	Credit Cards Summary
2				12/30/00	Credit Bureau Copy

FIGURE F.1 Financial Planning Checklist

	7 Investments
	7 Investments
12/30/00	Portfolio Model
12/30/00	Record Percentage in Growth/Non-Growth
12/30/00	Investment Accounts Summary
12/30/00	401K Summary
12/30/00	Morningstar Average Matrix
	8 Business Interests
	Business Interests Summary
	9 Life Insurance
12/30/00	Life Insurance Summary - H
12/30/00	Life Insurance Summary - W
	10 Health Insurance
12/30/00	Health Insurance Summary
12/30/00	Dental/Vision Summary
12/30/00	Long-Term Care Summay
12/30/00	Medigap Summary
	11 Property Casualty Insurance
12/30/00	Home Insurance Summary
12/30/00	Auto Insu ance Summary
12/30/00	Umbrella Insurance Summary
	12 Retirement Planning
12/30/00	QFP Retirement Planning Assumptions to Reach Goal
	Defined Benefit Plan Summary
9/26/02	Social Security Benefits Statement
	13 Dependent Planning
12/30/00	Education Funding Summary
	14 Disability Planning
12/30/00	Disability Insurance Summary
	15 Estate Planning
12/30/00	Estate Planning Summary
12/30/00	Letter of Instructions Worksheet
12/30/00	Record Keeping Worksheet: Attach to Letter of Instructions
12/30/00	Safe Deposit Box Inventory: Attach to Letter of Instructions
12/30/00	Man's Will Summary
12/30/00	Woman's Will Summary
12/30/00	Man's Revocable Trust Summary
12/30/00	Woman's Revocable Trust Summary
12/30/00	Man's Irrevocable Trust Summary
12/30/00	Woman's Irrevocable Trust Summary
12/30/00	Charitable Trust Summary
12/30/00	Man's Durable Power of Attorney Summary
12/30/00	Woman's Durable Power of Attorney Summary
12/30/00	Man's Health Care Proxy Summary
12/30/00	Woman's Health Care Proxy Summary
12/30/00	Man's Living Will Summary
12/30/00	Woman's Living Will Summary

The left margin numbers (2) appear next to: Social Security Benefits Statement (9/26/02), Letter of Instructions Worksheet, Record Keeping Worksheet, and Safe Deposit Box Inventory.

FIGURE F.1 *Continued*

Document Location Summary

Keep these in your safe-deposit box	Or (other location)	For this long
Birth certificates	Financial Planning box (2)	Permanently
Citizenship papers		Permanently
Inventory of personal property	_____	While current
Living will(s)	_____	While in effect
Marriage and divorce records	Financial Planning box (2)	Permanently
Passports	Mary's office in/out box	Permanently
Military service records	_____	Permanently
Deeds	_____	While current; then to dead storage
Mortgages	Black file drawer	While current
Leases	_____	While current plus two years
Title insurance policies	Black file drawer	While current
Valuable jewelry	Mary's jewelry box	Until disposed of
Stocks and bonds	2 EE bonds in 2. Imp. Info	Until disposed of
Promissory notes	_____	Until paid; then to dead storage
Auto titles, documents	Black file drawer	Until sold
Business agreements	_____	While current; then to dead storage

Keep these in your attorney's office	Or (other location)	For this long
Originals of wills and trusts	_____	While in effect
Powers of attorney	_____	While in effect
Power holder		
Safe-deposit box key (spare)	_____	While rented
Combination to home safe or strongbox	_____	Permanently

Keep these in your desk or file at home	Or (other location)	For this long
Bank statements, deposit slips	Black file drawer	While current; then to dead storage
Safe-deposit box inventory	_____	Permanently; update as required
Credit card numbers	1. Notes	Permanently; update as required
Warranties	Office shelf	While in effect
Personal tax returns (1040) and supporting	File drawers	Six years; then to dead storage
Tax estimates (1040 Es)	_____	Six years; then to dead storage
Canceled checks for deductions	Office inside cabinets	Six years; then to dead storage
Records of tax payments	Office	Six years; then to dead storage
Records of securities held and other investments	Black file drawer	Until sold; then to dead storage
Records of home cost and improvements	_____	Until home is sold; then to dead storage

Keep these in a home safe or strongbox	Or (other location)	For this long
Bankbooks	_____	Until account closed; then to dead storage
Duplicates of wills, trusts, powers of attorney	_____	While in effect
Safe-deposit box key	_____	While rented
Coin and stamp collections	_____	Until disposed of
Life insurance policies	Financial Planning box (9)	While in force
Casualty insurance policies	Financial Planning box (10)	While in effect; then to dead storage

FIGURE F.2 Document Location Summary

210

Yearly Tickler	
First Quarter	
1 January	Data Gathering
2 February	Retirement Planning
3 March	Tax Planning
Second Quarter	
4 April	Dependent Planning
5 May	Investing
6 June	Investments (Equity) Cash Flows Ret,Dis,Nor
Third Quarter	
7 July	Real Estate & Other Investments
8 August	Life Insurance
9 September	Health (Disability, Long-Term Care) Insurance
Fourth Quarter	
10 October	Estate Planning
11 November	Tax Planning
12 December	Property and Casualty Insurance

FIGURE F.3 Yearly Tickler

Portfolio Model

Client Name

Total Available	$566,091				7/24/2000
Reserve	0				
Available to invest	**$566,091**			**Estimated Return**	**9.60%**

	Allocation	Amount	Earns	Ratio	Average
Growth	90%	$509,482	10.00%	90.00%	9.00%
Non-Growth	10%	$56,609	6.00%	10.00%	0.60%

Growth		Non-Growth	

Type		$12,345	Type		($12,345)
Large Value	3%	$15,495	Money Market Fund	12%	$68,954
Large Blend	28%	$161,208	Inter-Term Bond	0%	
Large Growth	27%	$152,811	T-Bill	0%	
Medium Value	15%	$86,363	CDs	0%	
Medium Blend	0%		Corporate Bond Funds	0%	
Medium Growth	1%	$6,295	Domestic Bonds	0%	
Small Value	0%		Int'l Bond Fund	0%	
Small Blend			Fixed Annuity/GIC/Fund	0%	
Small Growth	0%		GIC Fund	0%	
Domestic Equities	0%		Muni Bond	0%	
Int'l Stock Fund	13%	$72,945	Total Cash	0%	
Specialty Fund	0%				
Stock Options	0%				
Direct Ownership					
Leveraged Real Estate	0%	$2,000			
Gold/Precious Metals	0%				
Venture Capital	0%				
Total Growth	**87%**	**$497,117**	**Total Non-Growth**	**12%**	**$68,954**

Current Mix

Investment Style	Value	Blend	Growth	
Large Co.	3%	28%	27%	58%
Medium Co.	15%	0%	1%	16%
Small Co.	0%	0%	0%	0%
	18%	28%	28%	

Int'l Stock Fund	13%
Domestic Equities	0%
Real Estate	0%
Gold/Precious Metals	0%
Venture Capital	0%

Projected Mix

Investment Style	Value	Blend	Growth	
Large Co.	0%	0%	0%	0%
Medium Co.	0%	0%	0%	0%
Small Co.	0%	0%	0%	0%
	0%	0%	0%	

Int'l Stock Fund	0%		0%
Domestic Equities	0%		0%
Real Estate			0%
Gold/Precious Metals	0%	0%	0%
Venture Capital	0%		0%

Growth	0%		0%

FIGURE F.4 Portfolio Model

Client Master Buy/(Sell)

Name	Symbol	Mkt Value	Buy/(Sell)	Remainder
Schwab #1234-1234 IRA=H				
Deutshe Int'l Equity	BTEQX	61,987		61,987
Gabelli Asset	GABAX	33,384		33,384
Janus Fund	JANSX	33,504		33,504
Janus Worldwide	JAWWX	144,899		144,899
Longleaf Partners	LLPFX	27,893		27,893
RS Diversified Growth	RSDGX	38,576		38,576
Schwab Value Advantage		142,051		142,051
Torray	TORYX	57,449		57,449
Turner Midcap	TMGFX	52,777		52,777
Weitz Hickory	WEHIX	55,048		55,048
Weitz Value	WVALX	144,999		144,999
Schwab #2222-4444 RthCnv IRA=H				
Fidelity Growth and Income	FGRIX	30,919		30,919
Harbor Capital Appreciation	HACAX	19,489		19,489
				.
Schwab #0000-0000 =W				
Fidelity Cash Reserves		21,687		21,687
Fidelity Magellan	FMAGX	36,287		36,287
Fidelity OTC	FOCPX	56,616		56,616
TRP Equity-Income	PRFDX	58,155		58,155
Vanguard Index 500	VFINX	80,249		80,249
Cash		6,243		6,243

FIGURE F.5 Buy-Sell

Life Insurance Review

Policy cost per thousand =

$$\text{Policy cost per thousand} = \frac{(P + CVP)(I + i) - (CSV + D)}{(F - CSV)(.001)}$$

where,

F	=	Face value
CSV	=	Cash Surrender Value at end of current policy year
CVP	=	Cash Surrender Value at end of Previous year
p	=	premium
D	=	Dividend paid
i	=	(chosen) interest rate

[Change the values in the outlined box to change cost per thousand.]

F =	$	100,000
CSV =	$	1,116
CVP =	$	544
p =	$	787
D =	$	26
i =		8.0%
1 =		1

Cost per thousand = | 2.99 |

| ::: |

[Change the current age to change results .]

Insured current age   34

Cost per thousand   divided by Benchmark for age from table =

Value = less than 1, do not replace
Value = less than 2, probably do not
consider replacing
Value = more than 2, consider replacing

Cost per thousand	Benchmark		
2.99	2	=	Value

1.49 | **PROBABLY DO NOT** consider replacing

Front-end load (FEL Multiple from the table) evaluation:

If the FEL Multiple > Value, the policy is not heavily front-end loaded.
If the FEL Multiple < Value, the policy is heavily front-end loaded.

FEL Multiple	Value
9	1.49 The policy is not heavily loaded

FIGURE F.6 Life Insurance Review

Source: Adapted from Joseph E. Belth, *Life Insurance: A Consumer's Handbook*, Bloomington, IN: Indiana University Press, 1985, pp. 79, 82, 84.

	Benchmarks				
Age*	Cost per thous	FEL Multiple	Age*	Cost per thous	FEL Multiple
1	1.50	10	43	4.00	7
2	1.50	10	44	4.00	7
3	1.50	10	45	6.50	6
4	1.50	10	46	6.50	6
5	1.50	10	47	6.50	6
6	1.50	10	48	6.50	6
7	1.50	10	49	6.50	6
8	1.50	10	50	10.00	5
9	1.50	10	51	10.00	5
10	1.50	10	52	10.00	5
11	1.50	10	53	10.00	5
12	1.50	10	54	10.00	5
13	1.50	10	55	15.00	4
14	1.50	10	56	15.00	4
15	1.50	10	57	15.00	4
16	1.50	10	58	15.00	4
17	1.50	10	59	15.00	4
18	1.50	10	60	25.00	3
19	1.50	10	61	25.00	3
20	1.50	10	62	25.00	3
21	1.50	10	63	25.00	3
22	1.50	10	64	25.00	3
23	1.50	10	65	35.00	3
24	1.50	10	66	35.00	3
25	1.50	10	67	35.00	3
26	1.50	10	68	35.00	3
27	1.50	10	69	35.00	3
28	1.50	10	70	50.00	3
29	1.50	10	71	50.00	3
30	2.00	9	72	50.00	3
31	2.00	9	73	50.00	3
32	2.00	9	74	50.00	3
33	2.00	9	75	80.00	2
34	2.00	9	76	80.00	2
35	3.00	8	77	80.00	2
36	3.00	8	78	80.00	2
37	3.00	8	79	80.00	2
38	3.00	8	80	125.00	2
39	3.00	8	81	125.00	2
40	4.00	7	82	125.00	2
41	4.00	7	83	125.00	2
42	4.00	7	84	125.00	2

FIGURE F.6 *Continued*

Life Insurance—H

	TOTALS					
Insured						
Company						
Address						
City, State Zip						
Phone						
Policy Number						
Policy Type						
Term Riders						
Face Value						
Policy Date						
Age at Issue						
Premium						
Annualized						
Payable						
Dividend Option						
Reduce Premium						
Pay Cash						
Paid Up Additions						
Accumulate						
Additional Benefits						
Waiver of						
Premium						
Accidental Death					·	
Automatic						
Premium Loan						
Owner						
Beneficiary:						
Primary						
Secondary						
Loan Interest						
Purpose						
Agent Name						
Agency						
Address						
City, State Zip						
Phone						
FAX						
E-mail						

FIGURE F.7 Life Insurance—Husband

Life Insurance—W

	TOTALS					
Insured						
Company						
Address						
City, State Zip						
Phone						
Policy Number						
Policy Type						
Term Riders						
Face Value						
Policy Date						
Age at Issue						
Premium						
Annualized						
Payable						
Dividend Option						
Reduce Premium						
Pay Cash						
Paid Up Additions						
Accumulate						
Additional Benefits						
Waiver of						
Premium						
Accidental Death						
Automatic						
Premium Loan						
Owner						
Beneficiary:						
Primary						
Secondary						
Loan Interest						
Purpose						
Agent Name						
Agency						
Address						
City, State Zip						
Phone						
FAX						
E-mail						

FIGURE F.8 Life Insurance—Wife

Hospital Insurance Summary

INSURED		
POLICY HOLDER		
INSURING CO		
POLICY NO		
POLICY DATE		
ANNUALIZED PREMIUM		
PAYABLE		
ADDITIONAL INSUREDS		
AGENT		

HOSPITAL/SURGICAL	Daily	Maximum
Hospital		
Intensive Care		
Miscellaneous Medical Expense		
Physicians--In Hospital		
Ambulance		
Surgical Expense Schedule		

MAJOR MEDICAL	
Maximum Lifetime Medical Exp	
Deductible Amount	
Accumulation Period	
Family Maximum Deductible	
Co-Insurance Percentage	
Amount Insured Pays before	
co-insurance % goes to 100%	
Individual	
Family	

SPECIAL LIMITS & ADDITIONS	
Pre-existing conditions	
Nervous and mental	
In-hospital	
Out of hospital	
Alcoholism & Drug Addiction	
X-Ray & Lab	
Maternity	
Pre-admission Review Required	
Phone Number	
Private Duty Nursing	
MEDIGAP POLICY PLAN	

INSURED	
POLICY HOLDER	
INSURING CO	
POLICY NO	
POLICY DATE	
ANNUALIZED PREMIUM	
PAYABLE	
ADDITIONAL INSUREDS	
AGENT	
PHONE NUMBER	
PLAN LETTER A-J	
Basic Benefit	
Skilled Nursing Care Coinsurance	
Part A Deductible	
Part B Deductible	
Part B Excess (100%)	
Foreign Travel Emergency	
At- Home Recovery	
Extended Drug Benefit 1250 or 3000	
Preventive Care	

FIGURE F.9 Hospital Insurance Summary

Dental/Vision Insurance

INSURED		
POLICY HOLDER		
INSURING CO		
POLICY NO		
POLICY DATE		
ANNUALIZED PREMIUM		
PAYABLE		
ADDITIONAL INSUREDS		
AGENT		
PHONE		
Dental/Vision	Coverage Amount	Maximum
Preventive Care		
Basic		
Endodontics		
Periodontics		
Oral Surgery		
Major Restorative		
Prosthetic Repairs		
Prosthetics		
Orthodontics		
Deductible		

FIGURE F.10 Dental/Vision Insurance

Long-Term Care

	Daily	Maximum
INSURED		
POLICY HOLDER		
INSURING CO		
POLICY NO		
POLICY DATE		
ANNUALIZED PREMIUM		
PAYABLE		
Premiums will Increase as Benefits Increase		
Premiums will Increase only if rates go up		
for all policyholders		
ADDITIONAL INSUREDS		
AGENT		
PHONE		

Daily Benefit Limits	Daily	Maximum
Nursing Home (Company Approved)		
Nursing Home (Other Nursing Homes)		
Home Health Care		
Adult Day Care		
Inflation Protection		
Benefit Period	Years	
Nursing Home		
Home Health Care		
Elimination Period		
Nursing Home		
Home Health Care		
Home Health Care Coverage		
Custodial		
Intermediate		
Skilled		
Care provided by relatives		
Qualification for Benefits		
Your Doctor's Certification		
Company Doctor's Certification		
Inability to perform ADL's		
Prior Hospital Stay (Home Care)		
Prior Hospital Stay (Nursing Home)		
Pre-Existing Condition Waiting Period (Months)		
Exclusions		
Alzheimer's		
Mental or Nervous Disorders		
Other		
Miscellaneous Benefits:		
Respite Care (Pays for Temporary Substitute)		
Non-Forfeiture		
Death Benefit		
Restoration of Benefits		
Discount when both H & W Buy		
Other		
PRESENT COST OF LONG-TERM CARE IN AREA		
Nursing Home Daily Charge		
NAME		
NAME		
Home Health Care Agency Daily Charge		
NAME		
NAME		

See Vision for Summary of Plan Coverage

FIGURE F.11 Long-Term Care

Property/Casualty Insurance

Type	Homeowners	Auto	Umbrella
Name of Insured			
Insuring Company			
Company Address			
Agent Name			
Agency			
Agent Address			
Agent Phone			
Agent E-mail			
Policy Number			
Property Description			
Date of Issue			
Expiration			
Annualized Premium			
Premium Payable			
Co-insurance Clause			
Deductible Amount			
HOMEOWNERS			
1. Dwelling			
2. Appurtenant Structures			
3. Scheduled Property			
4. Unscheduled Personal Property			
5. Additional Living Expenses			
6. Liability			
a. Personal Injury			
b. Property Damage			
c. Medical Payments			
7. Inflation Protection			
8. Replacement Cost			
9. Theft			
10. Rider for computer			
11. Covenant for business pursuits			
AUTOMOBILE/MARINE			
1. Comprehensive			
2. Collision			
3. Liability			
a. Bodily Injury			
b. Property Damage			
c. Medical Payments			
4. Uninsured Motorists			
5. Underinsured Motorists			
6. Towing and Labor			
7. Rental Reimbursement			
8. Multi-Car Discount			
9. Automatic Safety Belts			
Annual Premium			
UMBRELLA			
Limit of Liability			
a. Each Occurrence			
b. Annual Aggregate			
c. Retained Limit			
Schedule of Underlying Insurance Per Person			
Per Occurrence			
a. Homeowners			
b. Automobile			
Bodily Injury			
Property Damage			
Annual Premium			

FIGURE F.12 Property/Casualty Insurance

Defined Benefit Pension

Employer		
Plan Name		
Plan Number		
Trustee		
Administrator		
Effective Date		
Plan Year End		
Eligibility	Min	Max
Age		
Service		
Entry Dates		
Benefit Formula		
Normal Retirement Benefit		
Early Retirement Benefit		
Early Retirement Age		
Normal Retirement Age		
Pre-Retirement Benefits		
Death Benefit Formula		
Disability Benefit Formula		
Participant Loans		
Plan Author		
Trust ID Number		

FIGURE F.13 Defined Benefit Pension

College Expenses

FAMILY DATA

Children's names		Age now	Age to start college	Years of college	Today's cost of college
A		1	18	4	10,000.00
B		8	18	4	10,000.00
C		10	18	4	10,000.00

INVESTMENT ASSUMPTIONS

College inflation: 8.00%
Investment return: 10.00%

Initial lump-sum payment: 0 *Set to 0 for flat payment schedule.*
Pay in for this many years: 10

PAYMENT SCHEDULE

Date	Children in college		Pay in	Pay out	Accumulated value
2000			15,099.46	0.00	15,099.46
2001			15,099.46	0.00	31,708.87
2002			15,099.46	0.00	49,979.22
2003			15,099.46	0.00	70,076.61
2004			15,099.46	0.00	92,183.73
2005			15,099.46	0.00	116,501.56
2006			15,099.46	0.00	143,251.18
2007			15,099.46	0.00	172,675.76
2008			15,099.46	(19,990.05)	185,052.76
2009			15,099.46	(21,589.25)	197,068.24
2010			0.00	(46,632.78)	170,142.29
2011			0.00	(50,363.40)	136,793.12
2012			0.00	(27,196.24)	123,276.19
2013			0.00	(29,371.94)	106,231.87
2014			0.00	0.00	116,855.06
2015			0.00	0.00	128,540.57
2016			0.00	0.00	141,394.62
2017			0.00	(39,960.19)	115,573.89
2018			0.00	(43,157.01)	83,974.27
2019			0.00	(46,609.57)	45,762.12
2020			0.00	(50,338.34)	(0.00)

Totals: 150,994.63   375,208.77

FIGURE F.14 Dependent Planning—College Expenses

Irrevocable Trust

GRANTOR: _____

TRUSTEE(S): _____

SUCCESSOR TRUSTEE(S): _____

DATE: _____

BENEFICIARIES:

DURING THE GRANTOR'S LIFE:	ART. & PAR.
All income to spouse	_____
Trustee right to distribute all Trust assets	_____
Power of Appointment	_____
"Crummey" withdrawal power to spouse of $_____ for _____ days.	_____
"Crummey" withdrawal power to children of $_____ for _____ days.	_____

FIGURE F.15 Irrevocable Trust

NAME:

UPON THE GRANTOR'S DEATH   **ART. & PAR.**

    All income to spouse   _____

    All income to spouse and children   _____

    Trustee may distribute income to
    spouse, children, or others or   _____
    accumulate

Spouse's right to withdraw

    Trust assets   _____

    Limited standards   _____

    Greater of $5,000 or 5%   _____

Trustee may distribute Trust Assets

    To spouse   _____

    To children   _____

    To others   _____

Limited Power of Appointment

    During spouse's lifetime   _____

    By will at spouse's death   _____

Other Provisions

FIGURE F.15 *Continued*

NAME:

MISCELLANEOUS PROVISIONS   **ART. & PAR.**

Beneficiary's right to change trustee   _____

Simultaneous death clause   _____

Charitable distribution to:
_____

Orphan's Deduction Trust   _____

Generation Skipping Trust   _____

Ultimate Distribution Clause   _____

Spendthrift Clause   _____

FIGURE F.15 *Continued*

Index